Praise for
The Lion's Roar

"It is a delight for me to highly recommend *The Lion's Roar: A Beginner's Bible Study on the Gospel of St. Mark*, prepared by James Hornecker and published through the Family Life Center International. It is very important for Catholic families and individuals to break open the spiritual food that St. Mark's Gospel contains. There is rich and easy-to-understand commentary as well as thought-provoking study questions that will help all who use this program. God will reward you for praying and studying the Scriptures most seriously!"
- Rev. Michael J. Sheehan, Archbishop of Santa Fe

"I am happy to recommend *The Lion's Roar* as an aid to the study of the Gospel of St. Mark for those beginning the study of that work."
- Rev. Thomas Doran, Bishop of Rockford

"In the sea of books on the Bible available, *The Lion's Roar* is unique. James Hornecker provides an exploration of Mark's Gospel that's easy enough for the novice and useful enough for the serious student, all the while using a rock-solid Catholic approach to Scripture."
- Jeff Cavins, Author and Host of *Life on the Rock*

"My hope is that *The Lion's Roar* will bellow in the homes of all families who seek to teach the Scriptures to their children, and in the hearts of all who desire to understand God's Word more fully. Here the Christian will discover a most useful and practical commentary on St. Mark's Gospel."
- Marcus Grodi

"*The Lion's Roar* is a powerful Scripture and apologetics tool for every apologist. I highly recommend it for individual and group study."
- Patrick Madrid

"I highly recommend *The Lion's Roar* for teen, family, and group study. This book will be helpful to every Catholic homeschool."
- Laura Berquist, Author of *Designing Your Own Classical Curriculum*

The Lion's Roar

A Beginner's Bible Study
on the Gospel of St. Mark

James Hornecker

THE LION'S ROAR

A BEGINNER'S BIBLE STUDY
ON THE
GOSPEL OF ST. MARK

JAMES HORNECKER

FOREWORD BY STEVE WOOD

Nihil obstat:
Rev. Charles V. Antonicelli
Censor Deputatus

Imprimatur:
Most Reverend William E. Lori
Vicar General of the Archdiocese of Washington

November 30, 2000

The *Nihil obstat* and *Imprimatur* are official declarations that a book or pamphlet is free of doctrinal or moral error. No implication is contained therein that those who have granted the *Nihil obstat* and the *Imprimatur* agree with the content, opinions or statements expressed.

Scripture quotations are taken from the Catholic Edition of the Revised Standard Version of the Bible, copyright 1965, 1966 by the Division of Christian Education of the National Council of the Churches of Christ in the United States of America. Used by permission.

ISBN-13: 978-1500924805
ISBN-10: 1500924806
First Printing 2002 by Family Life Center Publications under ISBN: 0-9658582-5-1

Acknowledgements

Steve Wood, thank you for giving me so much support in bringing this book to completion. Scott Lundy, thank you for being the first one to guide me through the Gospel of St. Mark. Dr. Andy Minto, thank you for teaching me not just about Mark but how to study this marvelous Gospel. Andrea, my wife, and Jacob, Zachary, and Catherine, my children, thank you for sacrificing so much for me to write this book, which has occasionally distracted me from spending time with you. Betty Heaton, Peggy Burnham, James Burnham, and Philip Cutajar, thank you for your editorial contributions.

Supplementary materials available from the Mark These Words blog at jimhornecker.wordpress.com

Dedication

To my father, the late Wendell Hornecker, and to my mother, Betty Heaton, this book is dedicated. I owe you a debt I can never repay. Thank you.

Table of Contents

Foreword

by Steve Wood

Thirty years ago I was a wandering pilgrim, entangled in the jungle that is the New Age movement. I had to purchase a Bible to study Christianity—the religion I was born into—so that I could move on from the Christian faith and advance to "higher states of enlightenment."

As she handed me my new Bible, the salesperson made me promise that I would pray before reading the Scriptures. I kept my promise. I prayed that God would give me understanding in reading what I had considered, up to that point in my life, a very boring book. As I started to prayerfully read the Gospels, I encountered much more than I ever imagined possible. I didn't just experience enlightenment—I personally met Jesus Christ, the Light of the World. My life has never been the same since.

What should Catholics think about reading and studying the Bible? Just a few passages from the *Catechism of the Catholic Church* will show that the Church strongly encourages you to discover the Scriptures. The opening declaration is that the chief purpose of the life of man is to know and love God. "In the sacred books, the Father who is in heaven comes lovingly to meet his children, and talks with them."[1]

The *Catechism* clearly says that "access to Sacred Scripture ought to be open wide to Christian faithful."[2] The Bible is not intended just for the clergy, or for a special few. Jesus said, "The words that I have spoken to you are spirit and life" (John 6:63). The Bible is a life-changing book intended for all Christians—*and for you*.

The *Catechism* also says that "the Church forcefully and specifically exhorts all the Christian faithful...to learn 'the surpassing knowledge of Jesus Christ' by frequent reading of the divine Scriptures. 'Ignorance of the Scriptures is ignorance of Christ.'"[3]

The Lion's Roar: A Beginner's Bible Study on the Gospel of Mark, by James Hornecker, will help you know God better and have a closer relationship with him. I can't imagine a stronger encouragement to read and to devour this book!

Throughout this introductory-level work, James Hornecker has been constantly faithful to interpret the Sacred Scriptures in the light of Sacred Tradition. He has carefully avoided trendy scripture theories that will be outdated in a hundred (or in ten) years. You will be spared all the doubting and doubtful interpretations that are so often found in modern commentaries. The question, "Did God *really* say...?" has gotten the world into far too many problems already (see Genesis 3:1). *The Lion's Roar* is a rock-solid, trustworthy, and faithful commentary. I recommend it to you without hesitation.

Who will benefit from this commentary? Anyone who wants to begin the adventure of Scripture study! Mothers, fathers, teens, homeschoolers, men's and women's small groups, and youth groups will all profit from studying *The Lion's Roar*. It would be ideal if families studied it together. That is what I plan to do in my own family.

Just remember to pray before starting your discovery of the Gospel according to St. Mark. Your prayer can be as simple as, "Open my eyes, that I may behold wondrous things out of thy law" (Psalm 119:18). Just make your prayer heartfelt, and get ready for the adventure of drawing closer to God through studying the Sacred Scriptures.

[1] *Catechism of the Catholic Church*, Section 104, quoting *Dei Verbum*, 21

[2] *CCC*, Section 131, quoting *Dei Verbum*, 22

[3] *CCC*, Section 133, quoting Philippians 3:8 and St. Jerome

Getting Started
The Lion's Roar

Of the people you know, who is the best Christian role model? When I did youth ministry, I frequently asked this question of teenagers. Most of the time they'd scratch their heads and eventually toss out some relative who "goes to Mass a lot." But it was clear from talking to them that they deeply desired to see someone they admired live the Faith.

They wanted to see that kneeling in church is a position worth aspiring to. They longed to see people be able to speak the truths of the Gospel with conviction and yet appear "normal." It's easy to buy into the idea that being a Christian is being "out of the mainstream" or "abnormal." They had a hard time believing the Church was believable, when they didn't see people living what the Church teaches.

To be a Christian role model, to inspire others to look to God, takes dedication to God. It takes dedication to prayer, to doing what's right, and to learning who Jesus is and what he teaches. After all, you can't give what you don't have.

This book will help you be a role model for others. To do that, this book combines an easy-to-use Bible study program with an easy-to-understand commentary on the Gospel of Mark. The commentary will give you the "so that's what that means" feeling. The study program will enable you to develop the skills to gain your own insights into the Bible. Together, these two elements will give you an excellent understanding of the Gospel of Mark.

And knowing Mark better means knowing what Jesus actually said and did better. When you know that, then you can live like him more. The more like him you become, the more you will love. And there's a lot of people like those teenagers who can't wait to see Christ in you.

I hope you find this book as rewarding to use as I did writing it. Below you'll find more detailed information about how to get the most out of this book.

The Lion's Roar

The book's title needs some explanation. In Revelation 4:7 there are four astounding creatures around the throne of God in Heaven. They constantly adore God and inspire others to worship the Lord. These four heavenly creatures have been traditionally linked to the four Gospels. The one with the appearance of a lion is linked to the Gospel of Mark.

The images of the lion and the lion's roar remind us that Mark's Gospel has a dynamic, high-energy feel. In it Jesus constantly charges about, making the Kingdom of God present in powerful ways.

The lion's roar also looks to the opening and closing of the Gospel. The Gospel begins with the roar of John the Baptizer calling the people to repent (Mark 1:2-8). Near the Gospel's close Jesus "roars" on the cross as he dies (15:37), ransoming us from our sins (see 10:45).

In the jungle a lion's roar is heard for miles around, letting all the animals know that the king of the jungle is near and causing them to scurry away in fear. Jesus is far greater than a lion, but in a sense he is like one. In Mark's Gospel, everything Jesus says and does becomes the Lion's Roar, declaring that the true King, the Son of God, has come. Instead of scurrying away in fright, huge crowds rush to Jesus in hopes of finding what they have longed for and been promised by God: a true and perfect King who will rescue them. Here we find the King and his Kingdom.

Who is this book for?

Hopefully you. You may know a lot or a little about Jesus, the Church, and the Bible. Whatever your knowledge level may be, the book in your hands can help you to understand Mark's Gospel and the Catholic Faith better. Whether you're a teenager going to a Bible study, a father of four, a homeschooling mom, or a seasoned citizen wanting to refresh your faith, this book can be beneficial to you.

What can this book do for me?

While Jesus grew up in the town of Nazareth he worked with St. Joseph in his carpenter shop. During that time Jesus and St. Joseph surely had many conversations. They must have talked about business and the concerns of the town, and most importantly, they must have talked about life with God. These discussions between the Son of God and this exceptionally holy man transformed their place of business into a school of Scripture. In St. Joseph's carpenter shop, daily life and the life of faith united.

This book aims to bring St. Joseph's carpenter shop home to you. Carrying on the tradition begun by Jesus and St. Joseph, this book provides men, women, and teens with an opportunity to harmonize faith with daily life in their own carpenter shops.

This book is for the people in the pew. It was designed for adult and teenage Catholics who want to know the Bible better. This book, this carpenter shop, will work with you to examine your life in the light of faith, so that you can see where God can make a difference.

The Parts of the Book

This user-friendly Bible Study divides the Gospel of Mark into 12 manageable units. The four parts of each unit are described below.

Introduction

An event from the life of a saint or a story welcomes you to the unit by building a bridge from the Scripture section to daily life.

Individual Study

Before starting the Individual Study, read through the section of the Gospel of Mark being studied. Then answer the Individual Study questions. Don't worry. Most questions are easy.

The whole point of the Individual Study is to help you see what the text actually says. This is a "must do" exercise, because it is easy to read Scripture and miss big things.

For those who are using this book in conjunction with a Bible study group, the Individual Study should be done before the meeting.

Shop Talk

Shop Talk is the suggested format for Bible study meetings. Hopefully, your Shop Talk meetings will resemble Jesus and St. Joseph's carpenter shop conversations.

Shop Talk has three parts: "Gathering the Wood," "Building on the Foundation," and "Applying the Finish."

"Gathering the Wood" begins with a prayer. The opening prayer can take any form: a conversational request that God bless the time, or formal prayers like the "Our Father" and the "Hail Mary." If you have the opportunity, open up with a rosary or hold the Bible study after Mass (e.g., on Saturday mornings).

"Gathering the Wood" continues with each person sharing his experiences about a particular theme of the unit.

The real work comes in the second part, "Building on the Foundation." Here the focus shifts to the biblical passages and their impact on daily life. Your comments and questions here build upon the foundation. Every building has a foundation. Jesus Christ has made himself the foundation (Mark 12:10). In the Bible we encounter Jesus Christ. When we come to understand and live the messages that God gives us through Jesus in the Bible, then we build on the foundation. By discussing the scriptural passages, you become builders. The goal is to build a thoroughly Christian life for you and your family on the foundation of Christ.

Each person in the group has an important contribution to make. Each person has tools (experiences, insights, questions) to apply to the wood (the Scripture passages). If a person withholds his contribution, the group becomes like a table missing a leg; if one person dominates the conversation, then the group becomes like a house with only one wall.

Shop Talk wraps up with "Applying the Finish." Here you summarize what you've discussed and look to the future, in light of the knowledge you've gained.

A closing prayer concludes "Shop Talk". Begin with the sign of the cross and a period of silence. Afterwards, each person says to God what he thinks he ought. Give everyone an opportunity to voice his prayer, but do not force anyone to do so. At the end, one person may say some closing words, and the group may recite some formal prayers together. Remember to always pray with your heart!

Explanations

The last part of each unit is the "Explanations" section. In your reading of the Gospel you will come across surprising statements and confusing actions. To understand them better, check out the "Explanations." "Explanations" gives you the meanings of unclear words and a deeper understanding of some matters that initially appear quite simple.

The "Explanations" list in bold the verse and a word or phrase from that verse. An explanation of that word or phrase then follows.

Example: 12:18 Sadducees. The Sadducees

are a religious party that judged the five Mosaic books (Genesis, Exodus, Leviticus, Numbers, and Deuteronomy) alone to be inspired Scripture.

This book uses the Revised Standard Version, Catholic Edition (RSV-CE). The RSV-CE was chosen because it is the most literal translation of the Bible available in English. If the words from Scripture do not appear the same in your own Bible, you simply have a different translation.

All Scripture references that appear without a reference to a specific biblical book refer to the Gospel of Mark. (See Appendix 2: Bible and Catechism References.)

By the way, "Explanations" usually does not try to explain the similarities and differences between Mark and the other Gospels. It is better to study and appreciate each Gospel individually before looking at them together.

How do I use this for a small group Bible study?

If you want to go through this book with a Bible study group and you don't already have one, you will need to do some organizing. Bible study groups need several things: a regular time and place to meet, a moderator to keep the discussions moving and focused, and people to come.

There are many ways to get people to come. You can make this book part of your adult or teen religious education program. You can place an announcement in your parish bulletin. You can invite people involved in a particular ministry at your church (for example, lectors or ushers). You can invite teenagers from the youth group to

come. You can even invite people that don't go to your church.

The key to getting people to come is to personally invite them. Individual invitations work better than general ones. When you invite someone, express a sincere interest in his coming. Pray for the people you invite. Remember, you may need to re-invite them to come back to later meetings.

Have an organizational meeting with the prospective members of the Bible study group. At that meeting, distribute books and finalize details such as times and places. In between the organizational meeting and the first Bible study, have the participants complete the Individual Study for the first unit.

This book works well for Bible study groups that meet once a week for an hour to an hour and a half. To go over the whole Gospel it will take twelve weeks (twelve meetings). This is almost as long as a school semester. Attendance at meetings is more likely to be consistent if the study runs concurrently with a school semester.

How do I use this book if I'm just studying on my own?

If you just want to do a study of Mark's Gospel on your own, the only part of the book that needs adjustment is "Shop Talk." The adjustment is simple. Using a journal, write down your answers to the Shop Talk questions. Doing this will assist you in your prayers and reflections.

Can this book be used for high school, homeschool, and adult religious education?

This book can be used as a high school textbook either in a classroom or in a homeschool setting, or as a course book in an adult religious education setting. It will be necessary to acquire the Leader's Guide CD-ROM for this book from the Family Life Center (800-705-6131). The Leader's Guide includes the answers to the Individual Study questions, an exam, and the answers to the exam. Teachers should be aware that a student who uses this book on a daily basis will get through it much more quickly than twelve weeks.

Is there a specific Bible translation I should use?

There is no copy of the Gospel of Mark in this book. You need to use your own Bible. We strongly recommend that you use a Catholic Bible. In the "Explanations," there are occasional references to the Old Testament books that are in Catholic Bibles but not in Protestant Bibles. (To see if your Bible is Catholic or Protestant, look in the Table of Contents for 1 Maccabees. If it's not there, the Bible is a Protestant translation.) We warmly recommend the Revised Standard Version – Catholic Edition. Some other Catholic versions are the New American Bible, the Douay-Rheims Version, and the New Jerusalem Bible.

What about Bible commentaries?

You will likely find it helpful to consult other commentaries on Mark, so you can see what holy men and women have said about these passages over the centuries. Naturally, some commentaries are more helpful than others. I especially recommend the *Ignatius Catholic Study Bible on the Gospel of Mark*, by Scott Hahn and Curtis Mitch. It's very thorough, reverent, and insightful. It also has the full RSV-CE text of Mark.

Another highly recommended commentary is the Navarre Bible New Testament, which includes the RSV-CE text, as well as many valuable spiritual insights from both ancient and modern writers.

Guide to the Gospel of Saint Mark

There are a few things that are really helpful to know when you study Mark – things like what a Gospel is, who wrote it, when, and what are the best tips for understanding it. The following pages will give you these things.

What's a Gospel?

The word "Gospel" means "Good Message" or "Good News." The Gospel is the Good News of Jesus Christ, the Son of God. The Good News is the message Jesus brought through his words and deeds. But Jesus was not simply God's messenger, but God himself who became man so that we could know God more intimately, more perfectly, and more certainly.

Four of the Bible's 73 books focus exclusively on Jesus' life, death, and resurrection. We call these four books (Matthew, Mark, Luke, and John) the Gospels. The Gospels are the most treasured books of the Bible, because they relay to us the life of Jesus Christ more than any other biblical book.

Even though we commonly say there are four Gospels, in truth there is only one Gospel, which is simply the good news of Jesus Christ. The four Gospels are four written renditions of this one Gospel. Each of the four takes a different approach in presenting the Gospel, but the same Gospel is presented in each one. That's why the Gospels are often referred to as "The Gospel according to St. Matthew" (or St. Mark, St. Luke, or St. John). Calling one of them "Mark" or the "Gospel of Mark" is simply an abbreviation.

Since Jesus is the peak of God's revelation (*Catechism of the Catholic Church* 65, 73) and the Gospels are the most important witnesses to his life on earth, the study of the Gospels is an indispensable part of our knowledge of God and our relationship with him.

Let me give you an analogy. We are not content to simply know about our earthly father, we want to know him. We want to eat with him, talk with him, work with him, and just spend time with him. Through all this, we get to know him.

So we should not be content to just learn about God, our Heavenly Father. We must know him. We must talk to him in prayer. We must work with him as our lives are changed by his life. We must eat with him at our tables, and eat with him at the Table – at the altar of the Eucharist.

If we don't spend this time with him, then reading the Bible is in vain. Studying the Scriptures is worthless unless it is part of a growing relationship with the Lord.

All this led the Second Vatican Council to state in the *Dogmatic Constitution on Divine Revelation*, 25: " {The Council} earnestly and especially urges all the Christian faithful . . . to learn by frequent reading of the divine Scriptures 'the surpassing knowledge of Jesus Christ' (Philippians 3:8). 'For ignorance of the scriptures is ignorance of Christ' (St. Jerome). Therefore they should gladly go to the sacred text itself, whether in the liturgy, rich in the divine words, or in spiritual reading. . . . Let them remember that prayer should accompany the reading of sacred Scripture, so that God and man may talk together; for 'we speak to him when we pray; we hear him when we read the divine sayings' (St. Ambrose)."

Since it is good to take things one at a time, we specifically want to look at just one of the Gospels: the Gospel according to St. Mark.

Why Mark? Mark is a terrific Gospel to study because it is the shortest, easiest, and most dynamic of the four.

Who was Mark?

The early Church Fathers identify the author of the Gospel of Mark with John Mark, who appears several times in the pages of the New Testament. Here's what the New Testament tells us about Mark.

Acts 12:12 identifies him as the son of a woman named Mary, a wealthy widow in Jerusalem who owned a house where the first Christians often gathered to pray. This may have been the house where the Last Supper and the descent of the Holy Spirit at Pentecost took place. If that's the case, then Mark probably met Jesus before he was crucified. In fact, many people think that the unusual reference to a young man in Mark 14:51-52 refers to Mark.

Mark had a relative named Barnabas who was a close associate of St. Paul. Mark joined Paul and Barnabas (Acts 12:25) on Paul's first missionary journey. During that journey, Mark left them and returned to Jerusalem (Acts 13:13). When Paul and Barnabas were planning their second missionary journey (Acts 15:36-39), Barnabas wanted Mark to rejoin them, but Paul adamantly refused as he considered Mark's return to Jerusalem a desertion. Barnabas and Paul disagreed on this point so vehemently that they decided to go on separate journeys. So Mark went with Barnabas to Cyprus. But later on, Scripture doesn't tell us when, Paul and Mark made peace.

In Colossians 4:10 and Philemon 24, Paul tells us that Mark is with him. In fact, in the former reference he recommends Mark to the church in Colossae. In 2 Timothy 4:11, Paul asks Timothy to bring Mark to him because he is so useful in ministry. Mark has clearly become more reliable than he once was.

At another time, Mark turns up in Rome with St. Peter, under whom he had become a dear disciple. While in Rome, Peter even calls him "my son" (1 Peter 5:13). This relationship between Peter and Mark will prove to be very important for this Gospel.

Historical traditions give us more knowledge about St. Mark. St. Peter sent him to Alexandria, Egypt, and he became the bishop there. He was eventually martyred on April 25, 68 A.D., in the nearby town of Bucoli. The Church celebrates April 25 as St. Mark's feast day.

In the year 825, some men from Venice, Italy, traveled to Alexandria and obtained Mark's remains so they could bring them back to Venice. At the time, Egypt was under Muslim rule and was quite hostile to Christians. In order to get

Mark's remains past the customs officials, the Venetians covered the coffin with pork, which Muslims consider to be unholy. Customs saw the pork and gave the coffin a quick pass. When they got back to Venice, the people built a grand basilica to house the remains of the great Evangelist. The basilica still stands today and attracts many pilgrims each year.

Where did Mark get his information?

Since Mark didn't accompany Jesus in his ministry, he had to learn about what Jesus said and did from someone else. That someone else was St. Peter. When Mark was Peter's close disciple, many who heard Peter asked Mark to put in writing Peter's preaching about Jesus' life. The Church Fathers who tell us that Mark was the "disciple and interpreter of Peter" include Papias (2nd century), St. Irenaeus (2nd century), St. Clement of Alexandria (3rd century), Origen (3rd century), and St. Jerome (4th century).

The Petrine character of Mark's Gospel has been noted by many commentators throughout history. The outline of the Gospel matches up very well with Peter's speeches in Acts (for example, Acts 10:36-43). The famous Petrine quality of being impulsive shows itself as this Gospel speeds from one scene to the next, from one grand miracle to the next, rarely taking a breath, and often connecting scenes with the words "and," "then," and "immediately."

Another indication of Mark's Petrine origin - and a rather unusual one - comes in the consistent portrayal of Peter as the most arrogant and the weakest of the disciples. This portrayal demonstrates the humility he gained after he denied Christ three times on the very night that he said he was willing to die with him.

For more on where Mark got his information and the controversy about it, read Appendix 3: The Controversy about Mark.

When did Mark write?

Mark didn't say when he wrote, and the historical traditions regarding the timing of his writing differ somewhat. Mark probably wrote somewhere between 42 and 62 A.D., between 9 and 29 years after the resurrection of Jesus.

Upper limits for the dating of Mark have been established by the Vatican and by archaeology. The Pontifical Biblical Commission stated on June 26, 1912, that at that time there was no sound reason to believe anything different than that Mark wrote before Luke, and that Luke wrote no later than 63 A.D.

Among the Dead Sea Scrolls, archaeologists discovered a tiny fragment of the Gospel of Mark called 7Q5. Archaeologists have determined that 7Q5 came into existence no later than 68 A.D.

Despite these things, some modern biblical scholars say that Mark was written after 70 A.D. These scholars consider Jesus' prophecy in Mark 13:1-37 about the destruction of the Jerusalem Temple (which occurred in 70) to be a description of a past event, rather than a prophecy about the future. In other words, they say that Jesus never foretold the Temple's destruction but that later Christians said that Jesus did. They say this because some scholars are reluctant to admit that supernatural events such as prophecies about the future actually happen.

The opinion of such biblical scholars often has the effect of undermining people's confidence in the reliability of Mark and other biblical books. However, since the historical and archaeological evidence weighs against such a late date, there is no significant reason to go along with these scholars and believe that Mark was written after 70.

Where did Mark write?

Mark wrote in Rome for the Roman Christians who were eager to have Peter's preaching in writing. Many early Church fathers tell us that Mark wrote this Gospel in Rome for the Christians there. 1 Peter 5:13 supports this testimony.

The text of the Gospel itself points to a Roman origin. Although Mark originally wrote the Gospel in Greek (the most common language of the time), he borrowed many words from Latin (the language of the Romans). Some scholars argue that these Latin loan words don't necessarily mean the Gospel has a Roman origin, since the Roman Empire had spread all over the Mediterranean world and the borrowed words may have been used in many parts of the Empire. This is true. However, the other Gospels were written in other parts of the Empire, and they do not have nearly as many Latin words and Roman images. So the evidence weighs in favor of a Roman origin.

How was the Gospel of Mark transmitted to us?

The Church carefully preserved this Gospel over the centuries. The Church has always treasured it since it is a historically reliable account of Jesus' life, death and resurrection. The Church has likewise always considered it to be inspired by God.

After Mark wrote this Gospel, scribes and monks carefully hand-copied it. These copies are called manuscripts. There are many ancient manuscripts of Mark. Because Mark is a historically reliable account of Jesus, scholars study these manuscripts to make sure that we have the exact wording.

Scholars have found very few differences among the most ancient manuscripts. Most of these differences are very insignificant. Some, however, include whole sentences (verses). In other words, some manuscripts don't have certain verses that others do. Most of these "missing verses" are duplicates of other verses found in Mark or in other biblical books. It is important to know that none of the verses in question affect the meaning of the Gospel as a whole. These verses are noted as being in question in most modern translations of the Bible, as well as in the "Explanations" sections of this book.

It is reassuring to know that many more manuscripts of biblical books exist than for any other group of ancient writings. In fact, we are even more certain of the correct wording of Mark and other biblical books than we are of most every other ancient documents, even of writings as recent as William Shakespeare's plays.

What is the Gospel of Mark about?

Everything in the Gospel of Mark revolves around Jesus. However, Jesus is more than the central figure. He is the Gospel's revelation.

Mark's Gospel answers three critical questions. These questions figure into the meaning of virtually every passage of Mark. These three questions are the three keys that will unlock the meaning of Mark. They are: 1. Who is Jesus? 2. What does Jesus bring? 3. How should we respond to Jesus?

1. **Who is Jesus?** Mark gives us the answer in the very first line of the Gospel: Jesus is the Christ and the Son of God (1:1). Everything in the Gospel is based on this. But it's sort of hit and miss. People constantly try to figure out who Jesus is, but they miss the clues that Jesus gives them. If you remember that Jesus is the Christ and the Son of God, you'll figure out the clues more easily.

Not only the individual passages, but also the outline of the Gospel drives this point home. The first half of the Gospel culminates in the revelation of Jesus as the Christ when Peter calls him the Christ (8:29). The second half climaxes in the revelation of Jesus as the Son of God when the words come from a Roman centurion's lips (15:39).

But the reader is not in the dark waiting for these climactic revelations. Mark begins the Gospel by announcing that Jesus is the Christ and the Son of God (1:1). As the account of Jesus' life unfolds, it becomes increasingly obvious that Jesus says and does things that only God can do. In this way Mark does not just tell us who Jesus is - he shows us.

2. **What does Jesus bring?** The Kingdom of God (1:14). The word "Christ" means "anointed" and refers to the Jewish practice of anointing the king with oil. The oil symbolized the Spirit of God, who guided the new ruler. Jesus is the new ruler, the new anointed one, the new Christ. Jesus came to restore the Kingdom of David. But Jesus didn't come as a political ruler or as a military general. Instead, Jesus came as the king of the great Kingdom of God, which is first of all a spiritual Kingdom. The Kingdom of God is first concerned with the relationship between God and every person, and then concerned with the relationships between people.

What is the Kingdom of God? The Kingdom of God is the royal family of God (3:35). In this Kingdom we become princes and princesses of Heaven. The Kingdom is the peace that comes from being in a true and abiding relationship with God. The Kingdom of God is true and everlasting life with God (9:42-48).

It is also the re-establishment and fulfillment of David's Kingdom. The elements of David's Kingdom will be found in Jesus' Kingdom. Because many will look for David's political and military triumphs in Jesus' Kingdom, they will misunderstand and even attack it.

Entrance into the Kingdom comes by repentance, by faith (1:15), and by doing the will of God (3:35). To be in the Kingdom we must believe in Jesus and live his teachings.

The Kingdom of God reveals itself first in the ministry of Jesus (1:1-8:26) as he travels around Galilee teaching, healing, casting out demons, and drawing disciples to himself. Two prominent images of the Kingdom appear in this section: the image of the house (1:29; 2:1, 15; 3:20; 5:38; 7:24) and the image of the boat (3:9; 4:1, 36; 5:2, 21; 6:32, 45, 54). Through these images Mark shows us the Kingdom as the house of God and as intimacy with Christ on the sea of life. Both the house and the boat, then, teach us about the Church.

The Kingdom then reveals itself as the "way" to Jerusalem (8:27-16:20). This way (8:27; 9:30, 33; 10:1, 17, 32, 46, 52; 15:20-22) is the way of the cross for Jesus. It is also the way for his disciples: "If any man would come after me, let him deny

23

himself and take up his cross and follow me" (8:34). Anyone who would be in the Church must accept this way.

Along the way Jesus teaches his disciples the difficulties of discipleship and the suffering they must endure. He concludes his teaching by suffering death on the cross (15:37) and then rising to new life on the third day (16:1-8). So because of the resurrection, the way of the cross does not end in death, but in everlasting life. The way is hard, but the reward is glorious.

The *Catechism of the Catholic Church* teaches us that the Church is the beginning of the Kingdom of God (*CCC* 567). When Jesus brought the Kingdom of God into the world, it came to us in the form of the Church. We can experience the Kingdom of God most fully today in the Church: in her sacraments and worship, in the fellowship of her members, in the common struggle to live in union with God. Although elements of the Church (like the Bible or sound moral teaching) can certainly be found outside the Catholic Church, the fullness of the Church instituted by Jesus Christ is found in the Catholic Church (see the Vatican II document, *Dogmatic Constitution on the Church*, 8).

This connection between the Kingdom of God and the Catholic Church is visible in Mark's Gospel. As mentioned above, much of Jesus' work in bringing the Kingdom of God into the world occurs inside a house. But this isn't just any house. It's Simon Peter's house (1:29), the house of the first Pope. Essentially, Mark identifies the Kingdom of God with what would later become known as the Catholic Church, the Church governed by the successor of Peter.

3. How should we respond? The revelation of God always demands a response. We should respond

with repentance and belief (1:15). The Gospel is almost as much about the successes and failures of people's responses as it is about the revelation of Jesus and his Kingdom.

In brief, the content of the Gospel of Mark revolves around these three themes:

1. Jesus is the Christ and the Son of God.
2. Jesus brings the Kingdom of God to us.
3. Jesus brings us into the Kingdom of God when we repent of our sins and believe in him.

Keep these in mind while you read. Having these keys when you read Mark is like being a pilgrim instead of a tourist. You'll see things that the casual reader will miss. You'll see more clearly how to enter more fully into God's Kingdom.

Unit I
Jesus Appears With Authority

Introduction to Mark 1:1-45

You are invited to follow Jesus on a journey of spectacular healings, violent conflicts, intense love, heartbreaking betrayals, and revealing truths. Jesus' ministry opens with an invitation to four men to be his disciples. Jesus does not call these four men alone – he calls the readers of this Gospel as well.

Before you go on this journey, you need to know what Jesus - the journey's leader - is about. Who is Jesus? That's the main question of this whole Gospel. Mark doesn't leave us guessing. The answer comes in the very first verse: Jesus is the Christ, the Son of God.

The word "Christ" comes from a Greek word that means "anointed." Among the Jews, when a king was crowned he was anointed with oil and called a "Christ." Those "Christs" were shadows of the Christ to come. The prophets of the Old Testament spoke of a great king, a great Christ, who would come save his people. Jesus is that Christ.

Every year on the last Sunday of the litur-gical year, the Catholic Church celebrates the Feast of Christ the King. On that day we particularly honor the truth that Jesus is the King – not just of the Jews, but of all people and all nations. Jesus is the King of all because he is the Son of God. God created the universe and Jesus died for all men in it, so by divine right, Jesus, the Son of God, reigns over it.

When the Son of God became man, he brought the kingdom of God and an invitation (see 1:15). Answering this invitation means stepping into the kingdom of God. Answering this invitation and going on this journey will lead you into the truth about who Jesus is and what the kingdom is all about. The men who decide to follow Jesus here do so without hesitation, and they have not regretted their choice.

As you read the opening chapter of Mark, think about Jesus' kingship and the kingdom of God. See how the King wields his authority. See how he combines strong leadership and humble service. As you read, ask yourself why you would want to follow this Jesus.

INDIVIDUAL STUDY
Read Mark 1: 1-45 and then answer the following questions.

1. In 1:1, what are the two titles that tell us who Jesus is?

2. When John the Baptizer preaches, what response does he desire?

3. What does John say is the difference between Jesus and himself?

4. When Jesus comes out of the baptismal water, what three things immediately occur?

5. What happens to Jesus when he spends forty days in the wilderness?

6. When Jesus preaches, what twofold response does he desire?

7. What does Jesus promise Simon and Andrew when he calls them?

8. What names does the unclean spirit call Jesus?

9. When Jesus preaches and casts out an unclean spirit in the synagogue, how do the people respond?

10. What prompts Jesus to heal Simon's mother-in-law?

11. How does Simon's mother-in-law respond to being healed?

12. Why does Jesus not permit the demons to speak?

13. Where and when does Jesus pray?

14. When the healed leper disobeys Jesus, what is the consequence for Jesus?

SHOP TALK:

Discuss these questions in your Bible study group.

 ## GATHERING THE WOOD

(5 to 10 minutes)

● Begin with a prayer.

● Describe your most recent first day of work or school. What were your successes and failures? What did you do to prepare for that day?

 ## BUILDING ON THE FOUNDATION (40 to 45 minutes)

Reread each passage before discussing it.

The Ministry of John the Baptizer (1:2-8)

John's ministry is one of preparation. He prepares the people to receive Jesus by telling them to repent. How does repenting prepare the people for Jesus? What might John the Baptizer say if he preached to your town?

The Baptism of Jesus (1:9-11)

Jesus' ministry begins with him receiving his Father's blessing. What's it like for a son to hear his father call him his beloved Son? How does that prepare Jesus for his mission? What does this teach us about Jesus and the Father?

Jesus Calls the First Disciples (1:16-20)

These disciples leave everything behind to follow Jesus. Why might someone abandon his career for the chance to be with Jesus?

Jesus Preaches in the Synagogue (1:21-28)

Jesus teaches and casts out a demon in the synagogue. How does Jesus show his authority in this passage? How do the people respond to his authority here? How should they respond?

The End of the First Day of Ministry (1:32-39)

Jesus has a lot of success on this "first day" as he heals many and casts out demons, but he doesn't dwell on that success. Rather, he goes off to pray alone, and then moves on to other towns to minister there. How can success spoil a person? What can a person do to prevent being spoiled?

Jesus Heals the Leper (1:40-45)

After the healing, the leper quickly disobeys Jesus' commands. So not everything goes Jesus' way! What is the best way for a person to respond to a setback?

 ## APPLYING THE FINISH

(10 minutes)

As you begin to meet regularly in a Bible study group, it is good to discuss each person's expectations. How can this group best perform the role of John the Baptizer and prepare you to have faith in Jesus or deepen that faith?

During the closing prayer, resolve to discover more about who Jesus is.

Explanations

The Gospel Begins (1:1)

1:1 Beginning. This entire Gospel is just the beginning. Jesus' ministry through the Church is the continuation. gospel. Literally means "good message." Jesus. "Jesus" means "The Lord saves." Christ. Literally means "Anointed." Israelite kings were anointed with oil (1 Samuel 10:1). The prophets spoke of a Christ who would come to save his people (Isaiah 61:1). Son of God. Jesus is not just a man but God as well. See *CCC* 464-469.

The Ministry of John the Baptizer (1:2-8)

1:2-3 Isaiah. This quote combines Malachi 3:1 with Isaiah 40:3. Isaiah alone is mentioned as he is the better known prophet. 1:4 forgiveness of sins. John's baptism includes the petition that God forgive sins, but this baptism does not wipe away sin. Jesus answers this petition with the sacrament of Christian baptism. See *CCC* 1223-1228. 1:6 John was clothed. John's food and clothing recall the prophet Elijah's (2 Kings 1:8). 1:7 After me comes... John performs the task of Elijah (9:11-13), which is to prepare for the coming of the Christ (Malachi 4:5). thong of whose sandals... This highlights the superiority of Jesus over John. Even slaves of the ancient world did not perform this task as it was considered beneath their dignity. 1:8 Holy Spirit. John's baptism expresses repentance and a desire to live according to God's ways. Jesus' baptism brings the forgiveness of sins and the very Spirit of God. See *CCC* 1262-1274.

The Baptism of Jesus (1:9-11)

1:9 was baptized. The sinless Jesus is baptized for our sins, not his own. This points to the cross where Jesus takes our sins upon himself (see 10:45). In this baptism the heavens are torn, the Spirit descends, and the Father calls Jesus his "beloved Son." When Jesus dies, the Temple curtain is torn, Jesus gives up his spirit (his breath), and a centurion calls him "the Son of God" (15:37-39). **1:10 Spirit descending.** "The Holy Spirit descended visibly in bodily form upon Christ when he was baptized so that we may believe him to descend invisibly upon all those who are baptized afterwards" (St. Thomas Aquinas, *Summa Theologiae* III, q. 39, a. 6, ad. 3). **like a dove.** Doves symbolize peace between God and man (Genesis 8:8-12). **1:11 a voice...** The voice is God the Father's (9:7; 12:6). **beloved.** The term "beloved" indicates Jesus is God's only Son and that he is destined for a sacrificial death (Genesis 22:2, 12, 16; Judges 11:34). The Trinity revealed here as the Father, Son, and the Holy Spirit are all present and active.

Satan Tempts Jesus (1:12-13)

1:13 in the wilderness... Jesus goes there to prepare for his ministry. This recalls the purifications the Israelites underwent in the desert (Exodus 34:28; Deuteronomy 8:2; 1 Kings 19:8). **tempted by Satan.** Jesus conquers Satan as he resists temptation. **the wild beasts.** Jesus' victory is over nature as well (see 4:35-41; 6:51; 16:18). **angels ministered.** Jesus' victory is accompanied by angels (8:38; 13:27; 16:5-7).

The Summary of Jesus' Preaching (1:14-15)

1:14 gospel of God. Jesus' mission is to preach God's message. **1:15 time is fulfilled.** John completes the preparations for the Christ. He finishes the Old Testament period. **kingdom of God.** The kingdom of God is made fully available through Jesus and his Gospel. The kingdom of God is the gathering of people by Christ into the Family of God. It is the fulfillment and extension of the Old Testament covenants. To respond to Jesus' invitation involves entering into this kingdom. The Church is the seed and the beginning of the kingdom. See *CCC* 541-556, 567. **repent.** Completely turn away from sin and do penance. **believe in the gospel.** In addition to repentance, Jesus requires faith in his words.

Jesus Calls the First Disciples (1:16-20)

1:16 Simon. He is later renamed Peter (3:16). 1:17 Follow me. A rabbi does not call men to be his disciples. Potential disciples ask the rabbi to teach them. Jesus reverses that order, demonstrating that his authority is greater than a rabbi's. 1:19 John his brother. John is called James' brother to distinguish him from the Baptizer (3:17; 5:37). 1:20 left their father. Only a king has the authority to call sons away from their father (1 Samuel 8:11).

Jesus Preaches in the Synagogue (1:21-28)

1:21 sabbath. The sabbath is a day of worship and rest. See *CCC* 2174-2176. synagogue. The synagogue is the local building of Jewish worship. 1:22 one who had authority. Jesus' manner of teaching demonstrates who he is, as he lays down his original teachings powerfully and with absolute certainty. not as the scribes. The contrast (and conflict) with the religious leaders begins with Jesus' authoritative teaching. It seems that the scribes focused more on opinions and uncertainty. 1:23 their synagogue. Jesus' coming reveals that these Jews have fallen away from Jesus. Consequently it is *their* synagogue, not God's. 1:24 Have you come... This can also be translated, "You have come to destroy us!" This signals Jesus' victory over Satan (1:12-13) and recalls how King David triumphed over his enemies. I know who... As a spiritual being he recognizes Jesus' divinity. 1:25 Jesus rebuked him. Jesus does not desire demons' testimony but men's. He also doesn't want people to know his true identity (1:1) if they are likely to consider him merely a political savior and not a heavenly one. If the crowd considers him only as a holy military conqueror like David, then they are more likely to try to prevent the crucifixion that Jesus must suffer. 1:26 crying with a loud voice. The loud cry shows Jesus' victory over the devil (9:26; 15:37). 1:27 amazed. The response Jesus desires is repentance and belief (1:15). What is this... Instead of wondering who Jesus is, they wonder at his words.

Jesus Heals Simon's Mother-in-law (1:29-31)

1:29 he left the synagogue... Jesus' move from the Synagogue to Peter's house signals the move of God's favor from the Synagogue to the Church.

Peter's home becomes Jesus' home and a symbol of the Church (2:1-12; 3:19; 9:33). Other houses (2:15; 7:24; 10:10; 13:34-36; 14:3) point back to this one. **1:30 Simon's mother-in-law.** When Jesus called Simon Peter he was married (1 Corinthians 9:5). It has been considered probable by many throughout history that, after he became a disciple, Peter and his wife forsook living as husband and wife in order for him to be more dedicated to the ministry entrusted to him by Jesus. Considering the rigors of ministry, normal married life would have been practically impossible. The practice of celibacy among bishops and priests imitates the practice of Jesus, who never married. (See also Matthew 19:12; 1 Corinthians 7:7). **1:31 lifted her up.** This foreshadows the resurrection of the dead (5:41; 9:27).

The End of the First Day of Ministry (1:32-39)

1:32 sundown. At sundown the sabbath ends, allowing people to carry the sick. Carrying is work, and so is forbidden on the sabbath. **1:34 would not permit...** See the note on 1:25. **1:35 lonely place.** Jesus often chooses to pray alone (6:46; 14:32-35). **he prayed.** Perhaps Jesus prays against the temptation to stay in Capernaum, where his ministry is easy. **1:36 Simon and those...** In Jesus' absence, Simon leads. In Mark, to "be with" someone is to follow him (3:14; 4:36; 5:18; 14:67; 15:41; 16:10).

Jesus Heals the Leper (1:40-45)

1:40 leper. Lepers observe strict regulations that separate them from the community (Numbers 5:2). **If you will...** The leper expresses faith in Jesus' ability to heal. Jesus heals when faith is present (6:5-6). **1:41 touched him.** Jesus breaks convention, as lepers are "unclean" and not to be touched (Leviticus 13:45-46; 22:4-6). **1:42 the leprosy left him.** Only God could cure leprosy (2 Kings 5:7). **1:44 say nothing...** See the note on 1:25. Jesus commands the people he heals to be silent, so that they don't do the demons' work for them (5:43; 7:36; 8:26). **show yourself...** Jesus is a Jew, and obedient to the Mosaic Law. He wants the man to do what is holy and just (Leviticus 14:1-32). **proof...** Jesus wants to restore this man to the exercise of the Jewish faith. To do this he must go through the legal cleansing so that others will accept him. Jesus' command to silence concerns the cure's origin. **1:45 spread the news.** Jesus can silence demons (1:25), but not man.

Unit II
Engaged In Conflict

Introduction to Mark 2:1-3:35

Mother Teresa listened patiently while the president of the Central American country gave a speech blasting the United States President, Ronald Reagan. After he had finished his sweaty condemnation, it was her turn at the microphone. Mother Teresa stepped up and calmly said, "President Reagan needs our prayers. And so do you, Mr. President."

She went on to say that it was impossible to effectively run a country when you could not run your own family. These words hit the president squarely between the eyes. She explained that he was failing as a father because he had not baptized his children. She exhorted him to have them baptized without any more delays. She then offered to be his children's godmother.

Like Jesus often did with the authorities of his time, Mother Teresa exposed their hypocrisy. But that's not enough. A way out needs to be offered as well. For Mother Teresa, that was offering to be the godmother.

Jesus often extends a way out to the Pharisees and the other religious authorities who oppose him. He asks them questions like, "Is it lawful on the sabbath to do good or to do harm, to save life or to kill?" The answer is simple, but too often they follow their pride rather than logic and the truth.

Jesus fights several battles in this section. Each clash with the scribes and Pharisees escalates the tension. Hatred towards Jesus intensifies so much that his opponents finally begin to plot his murder (3:6). Their total rejection of Jesus becomes manifest when they declare that Jesus' power - which they cannot deny - comes from the devil.

Despite the viciousness of the attacks, Jesus defends himself in stunning fashion. Sadly, this only causes their hatred to grow since they hate looking like they're wrong. They don't seem to mind being wrong. It's just that embarrassing moment of being bested that they hate.

The conflicts will eventually result in Jesus' death, but even then Jesus will rise victorious.

Read on and witness the conflict and the victory of Jesus Christ.

INDIVIDUAL STUDY
Read Mark 2:1-3:35 and then answer the following questions.

1. What prompts Jesus to forgive the paralytic's sins?

2. Where is Levi when Jesus calls him?

3. In defending his eating with sinners, what word does Jesus use to describe them?

4. Why do Jesus' disciples not fast during Jesus' earthly ministry?

5. What wrong idea of the sabbath does Jesus say the Pharisees have?

6. What does Jesus do that "saves life" on the sabbath?

7. What do the Pharisees and Herodians do on the sabbath that is wrong?

8. Why does such a large multitude come out to Jesus by the sea?

9. What three things does Jesus appoint the Twelve to do?

10. What are the names of the Twelve who are with Jesus?

11. Why is it impossible to cast out demons by Satan's power?

12. What sins will be forgiven?

13. What seems to be the sin of blasphemy against the Holy Spirit?

14. Who belongs to Jesus' true family?

Shop Talk:

Discuss these questions in your Bible study group.

Gathering the Wood

(5 to 10 minutes)

● Begin with a prayer.

● Jesus constantly does battle with those who oppose him. Conflicts are common in our lives as well. How are disagreements resolved at your work, home, or school? What good can come from conflicts? What bad can come from them?

Building on the Foundation (40 to 45 minutes)

Reread each passage before discussing it.

Jesus Heals the Paralytic (2:1-12)

The four men who bring their friend to Jesus have tremendous faith that Jesus can help him. Jesus' response to their faith amazes everyone present. How can our faith be of service to our family and friends?

Jesus Calls Levi (2:13-17)

Consider this passage from the side of the scribes: do you encourage your family to dine with people with bad reputations? Why does Jesus eat with them?

Conflict over Fasting (2:18-22)

Fasting is a spiritual discipline and a form of prayer. It is also a sign of mourning. Do you know people who fast? If so, why do they do it? Why would you do it?

Conflicts over the Sabbath (2:23-3:6)

The Pharisees have overly strict rules against working on the sabbath. Jesus shows that their excessive regulations are actually unlawful. What do you do, or not do, to keep the Lord's Day holy?

Jesus Establishes the Twelve (3:13-19a)

Like Jesus, almost all these men were killed for preaching the Gospel. People still oppose Jesus in his ministry through the Church. Why do some people hate the Gospel and those who live it?

Jesus is Called Evil (3:19b-35)

The religious authorities and some of Jesus' own relatives oppose Jesus. They produce silly arguments against him, but Jesus responds with firm, logical answers. In his responses, the love of God shines through. Has there been a time when you were opposed for holding on to the Gospel or for simply doing what was right? How should you respond when you are treated badly because of the Gospel?

Applying the Finish

(10 minutes)

As Christians you will find yourselves being slighted and even persecuted at times. How does studying the Bible prepare you to handle such moments?

During the closing prayer, ask the Holy Spirit to assist those, including yourself, who are enduring conflicts, especially conflicts between family members.

Explanations

Jesus Heals the Paralytic (2:1-12)

2:1 home. Simon's home is Jesus' home (1:29). 2:2 the word. The gospel (1:14-15). 2:4 removed the roof. The roof mostly consists of mud and thatch. 2:5 their faith. Jesus grants forgiveness in response to the four men's faith. My son. To enter God's kingdom is to enter God's family. your sins are forgiven. Jesus does not ask God to forgive the sins, but says this by his own authority, implying that Jesus does what only God can do. The Old Testament suggests that sickness results from sin (Psalm 107:17). 2:6 scribes. Scribes instruct people in religious and legal matters. 2:7 blasphemy. The Mosaic Law teaches that a blasphemer should be put to death (Leviticus 24:16). Who can forgive... Jesus can only forgive sins if he is God. 2:8 perceiving in his spirit. God reads the hearts of men (Psalm 139:1-2). 2:9 Which is easier... Both are impossible for a man, but it is easier to claim that sins are forgiven as it requires no external proof (Deuteronomy 18:22). 2:10 Son of man. The Son of man is the everlasting king from Heaven (Daniel 7:13-14). Jesus calls himself the Son of man to emphasize his humanity, while he speaks of his ability to do what God alone does. By doing this Jesus teaches us the doctrine of the Incarnation, that Jesus is both fully God and fully man. See CCC 456-483. 2:11 I say to you. Jesus heals by his word, proving he can also forgive by his word.

Jesus Calls Levi (2:13-17)

2:13 sea. The Sea of Galilee. 2:14 as he passed... Jesus performed these same actions when he called the first disciples (1:16-20). Levi. Matthew 9:9 calls him by his Greek name "Matthew." He becomes one of the Twelve, but Mark never calls him Levi again (3:18). **son of Alphaeus.** Nowhere else is Levi called this. Another disciple, James (not John's brother), is called the son of Alphaeus (3:18). As the first disciples are brothers (1:16-20), this suggests that Levi and James are brothers. **tax office.** Levi is a tax collector. Tax collectors in Israel are notorious for immorality. **2:15 in his house.** Levi's house. See the note on 1:29. **2:16 the Pharisees.** The Pharisees are religious leaders who lead the people to follow both the Mosaic Law and the many customs associated with it. **said to his disciples.** They are not yet willing to confront Jesus directly. **Why does he eat...** Eating with sinners is seen as toleration of their sins (Psalm 1:1). **2:17 those who are sick.** Jesus calls sinners, his dinner companions, "sick." Jesus is there to help them, not to tolerate their sins. **not to call the righteous.** If a person thinks he is good, he will not see any need for Jesus. Jesus calls those who know their need for him.

Conflict over Fasting (2:18-22)

2:18 John's disciples. John the Baptizer's disciples. **2:19 Can the wedding...** Fasting is inappropriate at a celebration such as a wedding. **bridegroom.** Jesus is the groom. His people are his bride (Ephesians 5:21-33). **2:20 bridegroom is taken away.** This refers to his death. **they will fast...** Fasting is associated with mourning (Judith 8:6). Christians regularly fast in remembrance of Jesus' death and because of sins which cause death (Romans 6:23). **2:21 No one sews...** Jesus is the unshrunk cloth. Israel is the old garment. Jesus comes to repair Israel, but they won't accept him, so the tear will worsen. **2:22 no one puts...** Jesus is the new wine; Israel is the old wineskins. Jesus is more than Israel can hold! **but new wine...** Jesus will make a new Israel.

Conflicts over the Sabbath (2:23-3:6)

2:23 his disciples began... Picking grain is work, and as such is unlawful on the sabbath and punishable by death (Exodus 35:2). But their actions are not stealing if they immediately eat the grain (Deuteronomy 23:26). **2:24 the Pharisees said to him.** The Pharisees finally confront Jesus directly (2:6-7, 16, 18). **2:25 Have you never read...** Jesus points to a scriptural example (1 Samuel 21:1-6) where the law of preserving life outweighed the ceremonial law. **2:26 when Abiathar was high priest.**

Perhaps better translated "by Abiathar the high priest." 1 Samuel 21:1-6 says Ahimelech was the priest and makes no mention of Abiathar. Abiathar was Ahimelech's son and soon after became high priest. Jesus here informs us that Abiathar was present at the event, and that he approved of David's taking the bread by his silence and later by his service to David. Jesus refers to Abiathar, instead of his father Ahimelech, in order to emphasize the son's authority. He thus makes Abiathar a symbol of himself. Abiathar exercised authority over the bread of the Presence, in union with his father. Jesus exercises authority over the sabbath, in union with his Father. **bread of the Presence.** This bread was put near the Ark of the Covenant every sabbath. Only the Aaronic priests could eat it. See Leviticus 24:5-9. **2:27 The sabbath was made...** The sabbath exists to assist man in holiness. What is "unlawful" are legal restrictions that impede holiness. See *CCC* 2180-2188. **2:28 lord even...** God is Lord of the sabbath (Exodus 20:10). **3:2 they might accuse him.** Jewish custom dictates that the only medical procedures permissible on the sabbath are those done to save a life or prevent further injury. Procedures to improve health are forbidden. **3:4 Is it lawful...** Jesus asks a common sense question to show that excessive sabbath restrictions harden a man's heart. **3:6 Herodians.** The Pharisees and Herodians despise each other. Their common hatred for Jesus inspires an alliance. The Herodians support the idea of Herod ruling over Israel (6:14-29) with the Roman Empire nominally above him, but, in their view, the Romans limit Herod's power too much. They fear any messianic movement that could cause the Romans to oppress them even more. **how to destroy him.** They plot to kill, and so do what Jesus teaches to be unlawful. This is the first plotting of Jesus' death (11:18; 14:1).

The Crowds Come to Jesus (3:7-12)

3:7-8 Galilee...Sidon. These regions cover the area Israel controlled at the height of Israel's political power. Some of these are Gentile regions, foreshadowing the openness of the kingdom of God to Gentiles. **3:9 boat.** See the note on 4:1. **3:11 Son of God.** See the note on 1:24. **3:12 he strictly ordered...** See the note on 1:25.

Jesus Establishes the Twelve (3:13-19a)

3:13 on the mountain. Moses went up a mountain when God constituted the twelve tribes of Israel as a nation (Exodus 19-24). **those whom he desired.** Jesus decides who will be his apostles. They do not select themselves.

3:14 **twelve.** This number recalls the twelve tribes of Israel. Jesus makes these twelve the foundation of his Church, the New Israel. **to be with him.** The essence of discipleship is being with Jesus. The disciples are the historical link between Jesus and those who could not be with him then. **sent out to preach.** They will preach his gospel (1:14-15). **authority to cast...** They even share in Jesus' authority. 3:15 **Peter.** Simon's name is changed to "Peter," which means "rock." The name change, and Peter's being listed first, point to his being the first "rock" Jesus lays down in building the New Israel (12:10-11; Matthew 16:18; Ephesians 2:20). 3:16 **Boanerges...** James and John hear the thunder (Psalm 29:3-9) of God's voice at the Transfiguration (9:2-8). Peter, James, and John are Jesus' special witnesses (5:37; 9:2; 14:33). Having three witnesses makes their testimony very credible (Deuteronomy 19:15) 3:17-19 **Andrew.** The first four, Simon, James, John, and Andrew, are called at the beginning (1:16-20) and witness his whole ministry (1:29; 13:3). **Judas Iscariot...** Judas is listed last because of his betrayal (14:10-11; 43-50).

Jesus is Called Evil (3:19b-35)

3:19 **home.** See the note on 1:29. 3:21 **friends.** The word translated "friends" also means "family." These people knew Jesus when he lived in Nazareth. They are linked with those in 3:31-35 but aren't necessarily the same people. **beside himself.** They probably accuse him of this because of Jesus' statements about himself. 3:22 **scribes...from Jerusalem.** Being from Jerusalem, these scribes give an "official" Jewish position. **Beelzebul.** "Lord of flies." This is a pagan god's name and is used here as a name for Satan. **he casts out...** They admit Jesus' power. 3:23 **parables.** See the note on 4:2. These parables illustrate the absurdity of the scribes' judgment. 3:27 **strong man's house.** This refers to Satan and his dominion. **he first binds...** Jesus gained victory over Satan in the wilderness (1:12-13). 3:28 **all sins will be forgiven.** The Lord is infinitely merciful! **sons of men.** By using the plural of "Son of man," the title Jesus gives himself (2:10), Jesus teaches that those who receive forgiveness will be in union with him. 3:29 **blasphemes against the Holy Spirit.** Ultimately, this is the sin of not repenting and accepting the mercy of God (*CCC* 1864). 3:30 **He has an unclean spirit.** Jesus equates the unforgivable blasphemy with calling the Spirit's work Satan's work. A person with such an attitude rarely repents. 3:31 **brethren.** These are not Jesus' siblings but male relatives. Jews refer to such relatives as brothers (Genesis 11:26-28; 14:14; *CCC* 500). 3:35 **Whoever does the...** The kingdom of God is the family of God. Membership is shown by obeying God's will.

Unit III

The Kingdom of God Parables

Introduction to Mark 4:1-34

This is a true story.

A businessman phoned his wife from an airport in another city. After delivering his message, he said "Good-bye" and hung up.

After he hung up, the phone rang. He suspected the operator was calling to say he needed to put in more money for the long distance call. He answered the phone and sure enough it was the operator, but she didn't ask for money.

Instead, she told the busy man that after he had hung up, his wife had longingly said, "I love you."

The wife was saying "I love you" to her husband throughout the whole conversation by her quiet devotion to him, but he didn't recognize it. In that last moment, when his wife's love was suddenly made known, the beauty of that love pierced his heart.

Jesus gives us several parables in this section. He speaks of ordinary experiences to teach something that is extraordinary. To the casual reader they will seem no more extraordinary than the man's phone conversation with his wife. To the reader who senses something deeper and risks a loss – like the man who thought he might have to pay more for the phone call – he will discover the love of God coming through these parables.

The parables may strike you as simple or confusing. Do not skim over them, because if you look deeply, you will discover that they are revelations of who God is and his love for you.

At the end of your study of these parables, I hope that you will stand like the man with the phone in his hand, remembering an unselfish love that he had not fully realized.

INDIVIDUAL STUDY

Read Mark 4:1-34 and then answer the following questions.

1. Why does Jesus get in a boat?

2. What are the four kinds of ground in the first parable?

3. What happens to the seed in the good soil that does not happen to the seeds in the other kinds of soil?

4. What does Jesus give to the people who are with him that he doesn't give to those who aren't?

5. What does Jesus say that the seeds symbolize?

6. What do the birds symbolize?

7. What characterizes people who are like the rocky ground?

8. What characterizes people who are like the thorny ground?

9. What three things do "good soil" people do?

10. What will happen to the things that are secret?

11. What does Jesus promise to the man who uses a generous "measure"?

12. In the second parable of the sower, what happens to the seed?

13. In the parable of the mustard seed, what creatures benefit from that tiny seed?

14. Why does Jesus only use parables when he teaches the crowd?

SHOP TALK:

Discuss these questions in your Bible study group.

GATHERING THE WOOD

(5 to 10 minutes)

- Begin with a prayer.

- Discuss this quote: "The highest compliment a man can pay you occurs when he corrects you."

BUILDING ON THE

FOUNDATION (40 to 45 minutes)

Reread each passage before discussing it.

The Parable of the Sower (4:1-20)

This parable describes how people respond differently to the teachings of Jesus. The good soil is not hard like the path, nor is it full of rocks, nor is it full of thorns. How does a person become "good soil"? How does a person avoid becoming one of the "bad soils"?

The Parable of the Measure (4:24-25)

What does this parable teach about personal effort in faith?

The Parable of the Growing Seed (4:26-29)

The seed grows by the power of nature, not by the power of the farmer. Faith is similar as it grows by God's power, not our own. How does this add to what the previous parable taught?

The Parable of the Mustard Seed (4:30-32)

The mustard seed symbolizes the Church. By the power of God, the Church grew from a few people in Israel into a body of believers that today has hundreds of millions of members throughout the world. How has the Church helped you in your faith? What do you love most about the Church?

The Conclusion to the Parables (4:33-34)

The disciples are privileged to receive Jesus' explanations. Jesus does this to guide them in the truth and correct their misunderstandings. The disciples are thus better equipped to guide others in the truth and correct those who need it. The Pope and the bishops are the successors of these disciples. What do you find attractive about having a pope, bishops, and priests? What do you think is difficult about following them?

APPLYING THE FINISH

(10 minutes)

Jesus wants to show us the kingdom of God. How are these parables corrections of the ways of the crowd (people in general)? How do you correct someone who needs it?

During the closing prayer, ask Jesus to grant you understanding of the kingdom of God. Pray for the men God has ordained to bring the kingdom of God to you.

Explanations

The Parable of the Sower (4:1-20)

4:1 boat. Jesus often teaches from a boat (3:9; 4:36-41; 6:45-52; 8:14-21). The boat is the "school of Jesus" and an image of the Church. **sat in it.** Sitting is the usual teaching position among the Jews. **on the land.** Literally means "on the soil." **4:2 parables.** A parable describes truth, using images from common experience. Its simplicity makes the kingdom of God more understandable. The parable's images are often symbolic and have multiple meanings. **4:3 Listen!** Jesus often exhorts people to listen to his parables (4:9, 12, 23, 24) because it is the first step in becoming faithful (Romans 10:17). **sower.** The sower symbolizes first Jesus, but also can be understood as the Church or the individual Christian. **4:5 no depth of soil.** Without depth the plant can only grow upwards, and so it is very unstable. **4:6 it had no root.** Without a good foundation it has nothing to draw upon. **4:8 thirtyfold...** Such an abundant harvest is unexpected, especially when the wasted seed is counted. **4:9 ears to hear...** Jesus urges his audience to think about what they hear so that they can understand. It also means that everyone should listen to him. **4:10 those who were...** Others besides the twelve ask him about the parables. **parables.** This is plural as each image may be considered a parable. **4:11 To you...** Those close to Jesus are in a privileged position to receive explanations of his teaching. **secret.** Literally means "mystery." A mystery is a truth that God reveals. A mystery (like the Trinity) is so profound that we cannot understand absolutely everything about it, but we can understand it to a degree. **for those outside...** This includes Jesus' opponents as well as the curiosity-seekers in the crowd. Jesus deliberately does not open up the mystery of the kingdom to everyone. **4:12 see but not perceive...** Jesus quotes Isaiah 6:9-10. Jesus seems to express a desire for "those outside" to not be forgiven. In the parable of the sower the seed does not make the soil what it is but reveals what kind it is. The soil needs to be prepared beforehand. God spent centuries preparing Israel to receive Jesus, but not all responded to God's preparations. The parables are like the seeds, showing what kind of soil the people are. Jesus says these hard words because his parables will expose the bad soil as just that. **4:13 Do you not...** Despite being privileged with the secret of the kingdom, the disciples show only partial comprehension (7:17-18; 8:14-21, 27-33; 9:9-13, 30-32; 10:23-45; 11:20-25). **4:15 these are the ones.** The different soils are different kinds of people. **the path.** The path is hard and will not let the word penetrate. **4:17 no root in themselves.** They receive the word with emotion, but only superficially.

The Parables of Light and Measure (4:21-25)

4:21 lamp. The lamp symbolizes Jesus, faith, and the kingdom of God. **4:22 nothing hid.** Jesus' identity as Christ and Son of God will eventually come to light. Faith will not be kept secret forever. The mysteries of the kingdom will not remain unknown. **4:24 measure you give.** The generosity of your response to Jesus' words will determine his generosity to you. **still more...** God will not be outgiven. **4:25 him who has not...** Like the path that did not respond to the seed, even that seed will be taken away.

The Parable of the Growing Seed (4:26-29)

4:26 kingdom of God. Only now does Jesus explicitly say that the parables are about the kingdom of God. This alludes to the fact that the kingdom is not revealed all at once, but progressively. **man should scatter seed.** The man can be understood as God, Christ, the Church, or the Christian. The seed is the word and the kingdom. **4:27 he knows not how.** Man cannot fully comprehend this tiny act of nature, nor can he completely understand the growth of the kingdom of God. **4:29 harvest has come.** The harvest is the fulfillment of the kingdom of God in Jesus' death, resurrection, and his coming at the end of the world (13:24-27).

The Parable of the Mustard Seed (4:30-32)

4:31 mustard seed. The seed's growth symbolizes the Church's growth. **smallest of all seeds...** This does not mean the absolute smallest kind of seed in existence, but rather the smallest seed within their realm of experience. **4:32 birds of the air...** The Catholic Church will have room for everyone and will be a sure refuge from evil. The birds further symbolize the kings of the earth who all are under the authority of Jesus' kingdom of God (Ezekiel 31:2-6; Daniel 4:12).

The Conclusion to the Parables (4:33-34)

4:33 as they were able... Jesus accommodates his preaching to his audience's needs and their ability to respond to it. This complements 4:11-12. **4:34 he did not speak...** Parables here are the dividing point for whether someone draws near Christ or stays away. The first step in drawing near is to expend effort to understand the parable. **privately to his own disciples...** The disciples need this knowledge, as they will carry Jesus' word to others.

Unit IV

The Power of Faith in Jesus

Introduction to Mark 4:35 - 6:6

Why do we concern ourselves with Jesus at all?

There are two reasons. The first is because he is God himself. The second reason is that Jesus can bring us peace and salvation.

Do we want anything in life more than peace and salvation? We fight for what we believe in, not for the sake of fighting, but for the peace that we hope will result. We all suffer from various ills and sins. We want a life free from the little deaths of illness, pain, guilt, and most especially from the death of our bodies.

Jesus comes to bring us peace and salvation. He begins to do so in this life and completes it in the next. He has the power to do so because he is the Son of God. The God who created the universe out of nothing can create peace in a restless heart. Jesus simply asks us to have faith in him and he will provide. In this section, we will see both the power of Jesus and the power of faith.

Jesus rebukes a storm and creates a peaceful night, but not by the faith of his disciples. They lack faith. Jesus calms the storm by his own power – as a sign for them to have faith.

Jesus casts out demons who ironically show "faith" – a "faith" that humans neglect to show. The man, once released from the demons, goes on to live a life of obedience to the Lord, telling everyone about how worthy the Lord is of their faith.

Jesus then heals a woman who shows tremendous faith in him, and raises the daughter of a man who likewise demonstrates his faith when he falls prostrate before him. For these people, faith becomes salvation – salvation from illness, salvation from death, salvation from fear.

Despite all these miracles, those whom Jesus grew up with refuse to believe. Their skepticism stuns Jesus. Consequently, he seeks out those who do have faith and he heals their infirmities. How firm must their faith be to stay strong in the face of the casual "faith" of their countrymen!

But what is the faith that Jesus seeks? He seeks a faith that completely trusts that God provides and protects. He seeks a faith that believes that Jesus is the Son of God more strongly than a man believes in the finality of death. He seeks a faith that perseveres no matter what obstacle is placed in the way.

The faith Jesus seeks is not unreasonable. He gives many signs to demonstrate who he is. He gives all the evidence needed for someone to believe in him, to trust in him. The Gospel of Mark transmits that evidence to us. In the life of the Church today Jesus still works miracles for those who believe in him. And there is abundant evidence in the Church today that shows that faith in Jesus does indeed bring peace and happiness.

As you work through this section, keep in mind Jesus' words to the father Jairus, "Do not fear, only believe."

INDIVIDUAL STUDY
Read Mark 4:35- 6:6 and then answer the following questions.

1. Where is Jesus when the storm breaks?

2. What two things does Jesus do after he is awakened?

3. Describe the condition of the man with the unclean spirit before he meets Jesus.

4. What does the demon-possessed man call Jesus?

5. Describe the man's condition after Jesus casts a legion of demons out of him.

6. What instructions does Jesus give the demon-free man?

7. What does Jairus do when he sees Jesus?

8. Describe the woman with a flow of blood before she touches Jesus.

9. What does the woman do when Jesus calls her forward?

10. Why do some people say, "Why trouble the teacher any further?"

11. Who went with Jesus into the room where Jairus' dead daughter lay?

12. What does Jesus do to raise the girl?

13. Name two similarities between the woman with the flow of blood and the daughter of Jairus.

14. Why does Jesus perform only a few miracles in "his own country"?

SHOP TALK:
Discuss these questions in your Bible study group.

GATHERING THE WOOD

(5 to 10 minutes)

● Begin with a prayer.

● Describe a person in your life whose faith has impressed you.

BUILDING ON THE FOUNDATION (40 to 45 minutes)

Reread each passage before discussing it.

Jesus Rebukes the Storm (4:35-41)

The disciples are afraid because they don't realize that the power of Jesus is greater than the power of the heavy wind. Their fear shows their lack of faith. Jesus is unafraid; in fact, he sleeps through the storm. Who is Jesus that "even the wind and sea obey him"? What would you tell someone who asked you, "Who do you believe Jesus is, and why"?

Jesus Gains Victory over Legion (5:1-20)

The demons make the man live in the tombs. They make him cry out and bruise himself constantly. When Jesus sends the demons into the pigs, they all drown themselves. The demoniac cannot be subdued by men, but Jesus can and does subdue the demons, and he restores the man who suffered from them. What does this passage teach us about demons? What does this passage teach us about the power of Jesus and what he wants to do with that power? Why do you think the people react with fear of Jesus instead of with faith in Jesus?

Jesus and the Two Daughters (5:21-43)

The bleeding woman and Jairus both demonstrate persevering faith in Jesus. What obstacles to faith does each one overcome? What obstacles to faith do people like yourself overcome?

Jesus is Rejected in His Own Country (6:1-6)

Instead of developing faith in Jesus, the people of Nazareth find him offensive. They are not open to Jesus' call to believe in the kingdom of God, and they are not open to the call to repent. This distresses Jesus, particularly since some of his own relatives oppose him. How open is your family to talking about religion and praying together?

APPLYING THE FINISH

(10 minutes)

Jesus dearly desires everyone to have faith in him. How can a person who wants to have faith in Jesus build up that faith?

During the closing prayer, pray for those people who have been examples of faith to you. Pray that you can be an example of faith to others, especially to your family.

Explanations

Jesus Rebukes the Storm (4:35-41)

4:36 other boats... These may be the ones who ask about the parables in 4:10. 4:38 in the stern. The one in charge of the boat sits in the stern. asleep. Sleeping shows his confidence in God's protection (Job 11:18-19). 4:39 Peace! Be still! Jesus calms the sea by his own power, using the same words (in Greek) that he uses to rebuke demons (1:25). 4:40 Why are you afraid?... Faith in God brings security. Fear comes from trusting in human power, since human power is limited. 4:41 Who... The disciples finally wonder who Jesus is. wind and sea obey. God has power over the storm (Psalms 89:8-9).

Jesus Gains Victory over Legion (5:1-20)

5:1 country of the Gerasenes. This is Gentile territory. 5:2 tombs. Demons often associate themselves with death. 5:5 always crying out... The man's life is a living death. 5:6 worshiped him. Literally translated, "went down on his knees." The demons' "worship" is an attempt to prevent their destruction. 5:7 What have you... See the note on 1:24. Most High God. "Most High God" is used by Gentiles to reverently speak of God (Genesis 14:19; Daniel 3:26). This foreshadows the Gentiles' acceptance of Jesus. I adjure you... The demons call upon God to restrain Jesus from sending them to Hell. The Name of God is powerful and demons do not refrain from using it to serve themselves. **5:9 Legion.** A Roman Legion has up to 6,000 soldiers. **5:10 not to send them...** Spirits are often associated with geographic areas. Sending them out means sending them to Hell. **5:11 herd of swine.** Swine are "unclean" animals (Leviticus 11:7). **5:12 Send us to the swine.** Demons desire to be in a body so they can torment another being. **5:13 drowned.** The demons' association with death ends in the pigs' deaths. The demons suffer the destruction they wished to avoid. Drowning is associated with condemnation to hell (9:42; 11:23). **5:14 herdsmen fled...** Having both witnessed a stunning event and suffered a financial loss, the herdsmen quickly spread the news of Jesus' deed. **5:15 sitting there...** The man whom no one could bind (5:3) is tamed by Jesus. Being clothed shows his return to dignity. **they were afraid.** They realize Jesus' power is greater than Legion's, but instead of believing in him they fear what Jesus could do to them. **5:18 he might be with him.** The man desires to become one of the twelve (3:14). **5:19 he refused.** Becoming an apostle depends on Jesus' call, not on man's desire. **Go home to your friends...** Jesus does not command silence but commands proclamation as he wants the Gentiles to learn of God's mercy. He is not concerned about a political messianic uprising by the Gentiles (7:29). See the note on 1:25.

Jesus and the Two Daughters (5:21-43)

5:22 one of the rulers... Jairus is an associate of the authorities who oppose Jesus. Jesus does not refuse to help those who are exalted in society. **fell at his feet.** Being prostrate is a position of total submission, petition, and worship (5:33; 7:25; 14:35). **5:23 My little daughter...** Love for his daughter leads the man to turn to Jesus. **5:25 woman.** The woman is unnamed. Her position in society is at the opposite extreme from Jairus' elevated position. **flow of blood.** Her chronic hemorrhage makes her "unclean" (Leviticus 15:25-30), and so she was not supposed to be touched. **5:26 suffered much under...** The woman's ailment could not be cured by man (5:3). **5:27 came up behind...** Due to the nature of her illness, she fears openly approaching Jesus. Her faith in Jesus leads her to seek to be cured secretly. Touching Jesus while "unclean" would "contaminate" him (1:41). **5:28 touch even his garments.** This is not superstition. By faith she understands that the grace of God radiates from Jesus to the point of being present in his garments (6:56; 9:3). **5:30 perceiving in himself...** Jesus, not the garment, cures the woman. **5:33 fear and trembling.** She is afraid because she broke the ceremonial law and because she "stole" her healing. She fears his reprisals and a return to illness. **fell down before him.** See the note on 5:22. **whole truth.** She relates the story of her illness and publicly confesses her "theft." **5:34 Daughter.** Entering the kingdom of God means entering the family of God. **your faith has made you well.** Literally translated "your faith has saved you." **5:35 Why trouble the Teacher...** These people do not believe Jesus has power over death. They may be trying to prevent Jairus from losing favor in the sight of those who oppose Jesus. **5:37 he allowed no one...** Only those with faith will be witnesses. **Peter...** See the note on 3:16. **5:38 people weeping...** Mourning is not appropriate in the groom's presence (2:19). **5:39 not dead but sleeping.** "To men's eyes she was dead, she could not be awoken; in God's eyes she was sleeping, for her soul was alive and was subject to God's power, and her body was resting, awaiting the resurrection. Hence the custom which arose among Christians of referring to the dead, whom we know will rise again, as those who are asleep" (St. Bede, see St. Thomas Aquinas' *Catena Aurea* on Mark). If the parents obey Jesus' command to be silent (5:43), the people will likely think the girl was merely sleeping. **5:40 he put them all outside.** Their derision of Jesus disqualifies them from witnessing this miracle. **5:41 by the hand.** Jesus raises people by the hand (1:31; 9:27). **Talitha cumi.** Mark often gives us Jesus' actual words, spoken in Aramaic (3:17; 7:11, 34; 10:46; 11:9-10; 14:36; 15:22, 34). This effectively makes the reader a witness to the event. **5:43 he strictly charged them...** See the note on 1:25. This command dulls any positive impact this event would have on Jairus' fellow authorities. **something to eat.** Their proper concern is for their daughter.

Jesus is Rejected in His Own Country (6:1-6)

6:1 his own country. This is Nazareth (1:9, 24). The ambiguous phrase "own country" is used to allude to the rejection of Jesus by the whole Jewish nation. **6:2 Where did...** They cannot explain what they see and hear, so the Jews question the origins of Jesus' teaching and his miracles. They do not understand how this man, who they saw grow up, could be anything special. **6:3 carpenter.** This is the only place in Scripture where Jesus is called a carpenter. **son of Mary.** To call Jesus the son of Joseph here would dilute Mark's emphasis that Jesus is the Son of God. The people call Jesus this because Mary is likely present (Joseph is dead), and because they can point to her as his human origin. They fail to have faith because they do not look past Jesus' human origins. **brother of...** See the note on 3:31. (See also *CCC* 500.) The references to relatives point to their familiarity with Jesus' human origins. **they took offense...** They do not want to admit Jesus' divine origin, perhaps because that would mean they failed to recognize him earlier. **6:4 prophet...** Jesus is not honored as such by the Jews, but he is still a prophet (Nehemiah 9:1-38). **6:5 no mighty work...** Jesus does great works in response to faith. **6:6 he marveled...** God had done so much to prepare them for the Christ, yet they are still faithless. Jesus does so much to show them who he is, yet they do not repent. To refuse to believe Jesus in the face of the evidence causes Jesus to shake his head and leave to find others who will.

Unit V
Jesus the Breadwinner

Introduction to Mark 6:7 - 8:21

When groups of fathers are gathered and asked what it means to be a father, one very common answer is, "A father provides for his family." In other words, a father is expected to be the family's breadwinner. Even men whose wives earn more money than they do often say fathers ought to be breadwinners.

Of course, this is not the only role that a father plays in the family, but it is one that warrants serious reflection. After all, a family cannot survive without an income. Fathers especially take it upon themselves to fulfill this role.

Jesus brings the kingdom of God to us. Jesus has already shown us that entering this kingdom means entering the family of God (3:34-35). The Lord holds the position of provider and breadwinner in his family. As the members of God's family, we receive his good gifts.

In this section, Jesus shows us God's provision in many ways, but especially when he speaks of bread and eating.

Jesus begins by sending his disciples on a mission, commanding them to take no bread with them. The disciples have to rely on God alone to provide them with bread and other material necessities.

Jesus later works two miracles with bread. Twice he feeds massive crowds with just a smidgen of bread. These two miracles prepare us for the divine Bread God really wants to give us: the Eucharist, the actual body of Jesus Christ (14:22).

The many references to bread in Mark's Gospel teach us that God provides for all our needs. He provides for our souls through teachings and miracles. He provides for our bodies through bread and other gifts in order to sustain us and turn us back to the Provider.

That last point is important. In a family, the father does not seek to be an anonymous provider for his wife and children, but a man who is present to his family. He desires to love his family and be loved by them. God is no different. He wants us to know and love him. He wants us to be loved by him.

Read on and see Jesus the Breadwinner. See your father in him. Perhaps see yourself in him as well.

INDIVIDUAL STUDY
Read Mark 6:7-8:21 and then answer the following questions.

1. What does Jesus forbid the twelve from taking and doing on their mission?

2. What do the twelve do that is like what Jesus does?

3. Who do the people say that Jesus is?

4. Why does Herod have John the Baptizer beheaded?

5. What does Jesus want to give the apostles?

6. What does Jesus do with the five loaves and two fish?

7. How do the disciples react to Jesus when they see him walk on water?

8. Why do so many people want to touch Jesus' clothes?

9. What are the Pharisees concerned about when they approach Jesus?

10. What law of God do the Pharisees sometimes break when they uphold the "Corban" tradition?

11. What can defile a man?

12. How does the Syrophoenician woman get Jesus to grant her petition?

13. What does Jesus do to heal the deaf and dumb man?

14. How does Jesus respond to the request for a sign?

SHOP TALK:
Discuss these questions in your Bible study group.

GATHERING THE WOOD

(5 to 10 minutes)

- Begin with a prayer.

- Describe what it means to you to have (or be) a breadwinner in your family.

BUILDING ON THE FOUNDATION (40 to 45 minutes)

Reread each passage before discussing it.

Jesus Sends the Twelve on a Mission (6:7-13)

Why does Jesus give the Twelve such difficult restrictions on what they can take with them?

The Death of John the Baptizer (6:14-29)

As a ruler, Herod has a duty to lead his people faithfully. How does his unlawful marriage violate that duty? How should Herod have responded to John?

Jesus Feeds the Five Thousand (6:30-44)

Jesus provides teaching and miraculous bread for the people. How can a father provide for his family like Jesus does?

Jesus Walks on Water (6:45-52)

Before Jesus walks on water he spends several hours in prayer. How does prayer help a person? How does it help a family?

Conflict over Defilement (7:1-23)

Jesus teaches that people must concern themselves with having a pure heart. When you are tempted to sin or to break a commitment, what do you do? How can you avoid the things that can defile you?

Jesus Helps the Syrophoenician Woman (7:24-30)

Jesus is committed to offering the kingdom of God to the Jews first. But the Gentile woman wins him over by her faith, humility, and perseverance. Who are the people to whom you need to be the most committed? Who else needs you?

Jesus Feeds the Four Thousand (8:1-10)

Jesus again feeds a large crowd until they are satisfied. Why is it hard for people to expect God to provide for their needs?

Jesus Teaches About Bread (8:14-21)

Jesus emphasizes that he provides for his listeners abundantly. He teaches them that they have no need of the teaching of evil men. Are you finding Jesus' words and deeds to be food for your soul, or not?

APPLYING THE FINISH

(10 minutes)

How is Jesus a "breadwinner"?

During the closing prayer, remember those people who have been providers for you. Pray that Jesus will give you his "Bread" to eat.

Explanations

Jesus Sends the Twelve on a Mission (6:6-13)

6:7 two by two. Jesus called them two by two (1:16-20). Now he sends them out that way. Fellowship is part of the Gospel (11:1; 14:3). authority over... See the note on 3:15. 6:8 staff. A staff symbolizes the authority Jesus gives them. no bread... They are to rely on God to meet their needs. 6:10 Where you enter... This rule prevents them from moving to richer houses in the places where they gain acceptance. 6:11 will not receive you... To accept the apostles is to accept Jesus. shake off the dust... Doing this demonstrates their (and Jesus') complete separation from the town. 6:12 men should repent. Their message is Jesus' message (1:15). 6:13 anointed with oil... This anointing is the forerunner to the Sacrament of the Anointing of the Sick (James 5:14-15; CCC 1511).

The Death of John the Baptizer (6:14-29)

6:14 Some said... The crowd finally asks the question, "Who is Jesus?" 6:16 Herod heard... Herod's identification of Jesus with John suggests a guilty conscience and wishful thinking. 6:17 Herodias. Herod was seduced by Herodias. Herodias left her husband Philip, Herod's half-brother, to marry Herod – who was already married. 6:18 not lawful... Leviticus 18:16 forbids this. John will be killed for upholding marital purity. 6:20 Herod feared John... John's holiness attracts Herod, but Herod puts off becoming holy because he fears losing his unlawful wife. 6:22 Herodias' daughter... Her dance excites Herod's lust. Herodias' sins lead her to sacrifice her daughter to her husband's lust. **6:23 Whatever you ask...** See Esther 5:3 for a similar vow. **6:26 exceedingly sorry.** See Judges 11:29-40 for a similar regret. **6:29 laid it in a tomb.** John's death and burial foreshadows Jesus' death and burial (15:37-47).

Jesus Feeds the Five Thousand (6:30-44)

6:30 apostles. An apostle is one who is sent (3:13-19). **6:34 sheep without...** The people hunger spiritually. Those in charge of them (the Pharisees and others) do not give them what they need, so Jesus gives them his teachings. **6:37 You give them...** Jesus commissions the apostles to be concerned about the people's material needs. **two hundred denarii.** About two hundred days' wages. **6:39 sit down by companies.** Israel traveled in tribes, or companies, when God gave them manna (bread) from Heaven (Exodus 16:13-36). **green grass.** It is early spring, the time of the Jewish Feast of Unleavened Bread. **6:41 two fish.** A fish is a symbol for Christ. The first letter of each word "Jesus Christ, Son of God, Savior" in Greek spells the Greek word for fish. **he looked up...** Jesus will use similar actions during his Last Supper (14:22-25). **gave them to...** This fulfills his command to the disciples to give them something to eat. The apostles will come to feed the people by both the teaching of Jesus and the bread of the Eucharist, which is the Body of Jesus (14:22). **6:42 satisfied.** The satisfaction of bodies and souls is found in God (1 Kings 17:8-16; 2 Kings 4:42-44). **6:43 twelve baskets.** "Twelve" signifies the twelve tribes of Israel and the twelve apostles. The bread is treasured and not thrown away because it comes from Heaven. The Bread of Jesus (the Eucharist) will be the sign of the New Israel.

Jesus Walks on Water (6:45-52)

6:48 fourth watch. Between 3:00 a.m. and 6:00 a.m. **He meant to pass...** This suggests that Jesus wants them to follow him on the water. It also recalls Moses seeing God after he passed by (Exodus 33:19-34:7), as this event shows Jesus' divinity. **6:50 it is I.** This is the divine name revealed by God to

Moses (Exodus 3:14). **6:51 he got into...** If Jesus intended to go by foot to Bethsaida (6:45), he abandons that mission when he gets in the boat. **6:52 did not understand...** The loaves showed Jesus' divine origin. Had they understood that, they would have had faith when they saw Jesus walk on water. **hearts were hardened.** The disciples are still too set in their expectations of what the Christ should be like to recognize Jesus as the Christ (4:4).

Jesus Heals Many (6:53-56)

6:53 Gennesaret. Instead of going to Bethsaida (6:45), they go to Gennesaret. This means discontinuing Jesus' plan for rest for the disciples (6:31) in favor of continuing his ministry. **6:56 touch even the fringe...** See the note on 5:28.

Conflict over Defilement (7:1-23)

7:2 some of his disciples. One can assume his disciples do not wash because Jesus told them not to. **7:3 tradition of the elders.** This practice has its beginnings in the Mosaic Law (Exodus 30:19-21; Numbers 8:5-22; 18:8-13), which is from God, but is expanded by the Jewish rabbis. This particular tradition of washing comes from men, not God. **7:5 tradition of the elders.** The Pharisees admit the tradition is from men, but they consider violations of it to be violations of God's law. **7:6 Isaiah.** Isaiah 29:13. **7:7 in vain...** Worship is in vain when it is merely external or when human ideas take the place of divinely revealed truths. **7:8 You leave...** They charge Jesus with breaking the elders' laws, but Jesus condemns them for breaking the laws of God in favor of man's laws. **7:10 For Moses said...** Moses spoke the words of God (Exodus 20:12; 21:17). **7:11 What you would...** An adult son is obligated by God's command to care for his elderly parents. The Corban tradition allows him to make an oath declaring that the amount (Corban) he would spend on his parents is dedicated to God. This amount is supposed to be given to the Temple; however, the Corban practice permits him to pay a mere fraction and so satisfy the vow. **7:12 you no longer permit.** To uphold the vow the man must never give material support to his parents. Numbers 30:1-2 binds a man to fulfill a vow he has made to God.

However, Numbers 30:3-16 teaches that exceptions are made when conflicts arise with other commandments of God. **7:15 there is nothing...** This teaching goes beyond the controversy with the Pharisees as it discontinues elements of the Mosaic Law (Leviticus 11:1-47; Deuteronomy 14:3-21) that teach that certain foods defile the eater. Jesus teaches that purity is first of all a spiritual condition, not a physical one. **7:16 If any man has ears to hear, let him hear.** This verse is missing in some manuscripts and so is left out of most modern translations. It repeats 4:9, 23. **7:17 parable.** Here "parable" means a teaching whose meaning is not immediately understood. **7:19 Thus he declared...** Jesus' words end the food restrictions of the Mosaic Law. **7:21 For from within...** Defilement results from the choosing of evil, because evil separates one from God.

Jesus Helps the Syrophoenician Woman (7:24-30)

7:24 Tyre and Sidon. These two Gentile cities are condemned often in the Old Testament (e.g., Isaiah 23:1-15). **house.** See the note on 1:29. **7:25 fell down...** See the note on 5:22. **7:26 Syrophoenician.** She is a Gentile. **7:27 children first.** The children are the people of Israel. Jesus' ministry is to them first, because of the faith of their forefathers and God's covenants with them. **bread.** The bread symbolizes the kingdom of God. **dogs.** Jesus refers to Gentiles as "dogs" because of their history of immorality and worship of false gods. **7:28 crumbs.** Her desire to receive grace from Jesus and her faith in him leads her to persevere in her request, despite knowing that she is unworthy of Jesus' help. **7:29 For this saying...** Jesus recognizes her faith in her humble, trusting perseverance. **demon has left...** Jesus casts out the demon without even being near it.

Jesus Heals the Deaf, Mute Man (7:31-37)

7:31 Decapolis. Jesus goes from Tyre and Sidon in the far north to the Decapolis, which is mostly to the southeast of the Sea of Galilee. This means he goes through a great deal of Gentile land, foreshadowing the Church's ministry to the Gentiles. **7:32 they.** It seems that Jesus ventures back to Jewish Galilee, where the crowd finds him again. **they besought.** The man's inability to communicate leads to the crowd's intercession for him. **7:33 he put his fingers...** These actions are done so that the man can see that Jesus is performing the healing. The actions give him confidence that Jesus is healing him. **7:35 spoke plainly.** That he knows the language enough to speak it is another miracle. **7:36 he charged them...** See the note on 1:25. **the more zealously...** The crowd is more interested in Jesus' miracles than in obeying him. **7:37 deaf hear...** The crowd recognizes that Jesus fulfills Scripture (Isaiah 35:5-6), but they still do not recognize Jesus.

Jesus Feeds the Four Thousand (8:1-10)

8:2 three days... The three days of having nothing to eat foreshadow the three days of Jesus' death (10:34). **8:3 long way.** These people are Gentiles. **8:6 given thanks.** The Greek word for "Eucharist" is used here (6:41; 14:22). **8:8 satisfied.** Satisfaction is found in Jesus (6:42). **seven baskets.** "Seven" symbolizes perfection, and so points to the miracle's perfection. The bread's preservation foreshadows the Eucharist's preservation in tabernacles.

Demand for a Sign (8:11-13)

8:11 sign from heaven. The Pharisees are not looking to believe in Jesus, otherwise they would already believe in him because of his many miracles. They do this to get Jesus to claim that he is sent by God, so that they can turn him over to Herod as a political threat (3:6). **8:12 sighed deeply...** Faithlessness pains Jesus. **this generation.** This is the people living at that particular time. **no sign...** This is not a refusal to work miracles but a refusal to be the kind of Christ the Pharisees desire - one that works miracles to show power and gain acceptance by those who are influential in the world.

Jesus Teaches About Bread (8:14-21)

8:14 one loaf. Jesus is the one loaf. **8:15 leaven.** Leaven makes bread rise, but bad leaven can spoil the bread. Jews often speak of evil ruining the world like bad leaven. **Pharisees...Herod.** They desire Jesus' death (3:6; 6:14-29). Their leaven is pride that cannot accept a humble, suffering Christ. **8:16**

We have no bread. The disciples do not recognize Jesus as their bread. **8:17 Do you not yet...** Jesus asks if they recognize the one loaf that is with them: himself. **8:18 Having eyes...** His questions recall his exhortations to hear his words (4:3, 9). It also foreshadows the healings of the blind men (8:22-26; 10:46-52) who gain both physical and spiritual vision. **8:21 Do you not yet understand?** By these questions Jesus teaches that he, himself, is the bread, and that he is more than the people are capable of receiving.

Unit VI
The Revelation of the Christ

Introduction to Mark 8:22 - 9:50

It took two touches for Jesus to heal the blind man.

Jesus begins the healing by using his own spit to anoint the man's eyes. But here is the surprising part: the man is not completely healed! Why not?

The man does see more than he could before, but that the man doesn't immediately regain all his vision is a shocking turn of events. None of Jesus' other healings was only partially successful on the first try.

What's going on here?

When the blind man is brought to Jesus he has little or no faith. He does not come on his own. Others bring him to Jesus. Their faith stands in for his.

But Jesus wants this man to have faith. So he pulls him away from the crowd. Then he puts spit on his eyes and lays hands on him. Why? So the man can feel that Jesus is doing something to heal him.

His faith (or the crowd's faith) is enough to begin the healing, but it is not enough to finish it. Remember, Jesus heals where faith is present, not doubt (see 6:5-6). Getting a little bit of vision gives him more confidence in Jesus' ability to heal. So Jesus lays his hands on him, and he receives the rest of his vision.

This healing is about our spiritual lives as well. We don't normally receive a complete faith all at once. It comes bit by bit. Jesus gives us special graces so that we grow in confidence in the love of God.

This healing points to our understanding of Jesus and his Gospel. We don't understand all of it right away. It takes us time to see who Jesus really is and who he wants us to be. In the subsequent passage, Peter calls Jesus "the Christ," but doesn't fully understand what that means. Peter sees, but he sees unclearly. The fullness of who Jesus is will be seen more clearly later in the Gospel.

Jesus has to "touch our eyes" many times for us to come to a good and holy faith, and to come to a firm understanding of the Gospel.

Jesus "touches our eyes" in many ways. He does so when we pray, when we receive the Sacraments, in events in our daily lives, and when we study his Gospel.

With that in mind, ask Jesus to "touch your eyes" as you begin this section.

INDIVIDUAL STUDY

Read Mark 8:22-9:50 and then answer the following questions.

1. What does Jesus do to heal the blind man?

2. Of the answers to Jesus' question about his identity, which answer does he accept?

3. What does Jesus say will happen to the Son of man, the Christ?

4. What is the answer to Jesus' question in 8:36?

5. What do Peter, James, and John hear on the high mountain?

6. Who came as Elijah, if Jesus says he already came?

7. What does the father of the demon-possessed boy say that prompts Jesus to cast the demon out?

8. Why are the disciples unable to cast out the demon?

9. What message of hope does Jesus give when he speaks of his death?

10. What direction does Jesus give to the person who wants to be the greatest?

11. If a child is received in Jesus' name, who else is being received?

12. Why does Jesus refuse to support John in forbidding the man from casting out demons in Jesus' name?

13. What does Jesus say about leading others into sin?

14. What does Jesus teach about Hell?

Shop Talk:

Discuss these questions in your Bible study group.

Gathering the Wood

(5 to 10 minutes)

● Begin with a prayer.

● The disciples gradually realize the truth about Jesus. Did you ever learn how to play a musical instrument, how to speak a foreign language, or how to play a sport like football? Did you learn how to do it all at once, or was it a process?

Building on the Foundation (40 to 45 minutes)

Reread each passage before discussing it.

Jesus Heals the Blind Man (8:22-26)

Jesus heals the blind man in two steps. The man symbolizes those who come to faith in Jesus in steps. If you were the blind man, would you be happy when you began to see, or would you be frustrated that you didn't see clearly immediately?

Peter Confesses that Jesus is the Christ (8:27-30)

How do people you know answer the question, "Who is Jesus?" How is Jesus different from other famous religious figures?

Jesus' First Prophecy of His Passion (8:31-38)

In a way, Peter's rebuke is understandable. If you knew a man with Jesus' qualities, would you want him to become President or to be put to death?

The Transfiguration of Jesus (9:1-8)

Jesus is vastly underrated. Peter calls him the Christ but doesn't understand what that means, so God steps in to enlighten him. How can you convince people who underrate Jesus to listen to him?

Jesus Teaches About Elijah (9:9-13)

One of Elijah's tasks is the restoration of the hearts of fathers to their children (Malachi 4:6). In what ways do children today need their fathers' hearts?

Jesus Casts Out the Dumb Demon (9:14-29)

The father's prayer of faith (9:24) is the key to saving his son. What role should Jesus have in the relationship between father and son?

Jesus Teaches About Greatness (9:33-37)

Spending time with a child does not usually advance a career, but Jesus tells us that the one who does so is truly the greatest. How can you be great today?

Applying the Finish

(10 minutes)

How did Jesus "touch your eyes" today? In other words, what do you see more clearly now than you did an hour ago?

During the closing prayer, ask Jesus to keep "touching your eyes" and showing you the truth about himself. Thank him for what you see more clearly.

Explanations

Jesus Heals the Blind Man (8:22-26)

8:22 people brought... The blind man comes to Jesus by the crowd's intercession (7:32). 8:23 led him out... Jesus builds up the man's faith away from the crowd. spit on his eyes. This gesture tells the man that he is being healed. He is anointed by the "oil" from Christ's lips (6:13). 8:24 I see men... He is beginning to see. This indicates that he once could see or that Jesus miraculously gives him knowledge of what he sees. 8:25 he laid hands... Now the man has enough faith to be completely healed (Psalm 119:18). 8:26 Do not enter... See the note on 1:25.

Peter Confesses that Jesus is the Christ (8:27-30)

8:27 on the way. The "way" becomes the new school of Jesus (see the note on 3:9). It is the way of the cross, as the "way" ends with the crucifixion in Jerusalem. On the way, Jesus teaches about who he is and the hardships of discipleship. 8:28 John the Baptist... The disciples report what is given in 6:14-16. 8:29 who do you say... Jesus wants them to confess his true identity. You are the Christ. Peter's answer is correct but incomplete, as there is no reference to Jesus being the "Son of God" (see 1:1). Peter does in fact call Jesus the "Son of the living God" here (Matthew 16:16), but Mark does not include this because Peter does not adequately understand what it means (see 8:31-33), and because Mark emphasizes that Jesus is revealed most intensely as the Son of God when he dies on the cross (15:39). 8:30 tell no one. See the note on 1:25.

Jesus' First Prophecy of His Passion (8:31-38)

8:31 **Son of man.** See the note on 2:10. Jesus calls himself this as he points to the human sufferings he will undergo despite being the Son of God. **suffer many things**... Christ's way is a way of suffering and death. This is the first of three prophecies of his passion (9:31; 10:33). **after three days**... Jesus' prophecy of his death ends with these words of victory (16:1-20), but the disciples focus on the suffering. 8:32 **rebuke him.** Peter thinks his emphasis on a glorious triumph is superior to Jesus' emphasis on a humiliating "defeat." 8:33 **turning and seeing**... Jesus rebukes Peter, making him an example to the disciples who share Peter's sentiments. **Get behind me, Satan!** "Satan" here means "adversary." Peter is called this because he opposes God's way. To "get behind" Jesus is to follow him, to not oppose him. Jesus wants obedience even when understanding is lacking. 8:34 **called to him**... Anyone who would be Jesus' follower must accept Jesus' way as his own. **take up his cross.** To the Jews the cross is a symbol of suffering, humiliation, and death at the hands of evil men. Jesus' followers are called to embrace this cross. 8:35 **whoever would save**... Jesus knows the cross is unattractive, so he gives these words of hope and warning. 8:36 **what does it profit**... Nothing can save a man except taking up the cross. 8:38 **ashamed of me**... Jesus is fair. **when he comes**... Jesus will return in glory at the Judgment at the end of the world (13:26-27; 14:62). See CCC 677-682.

The Transfiguration of Jesus (9:1-8)

9:1 **not taste death.** This event will take place before the last apostle dies (before 100 A.D.). **kingdom of God**... This is fulfilled in the Temple's destruction in 70 A.D. - only a few of the apostles were still alive. This event showed that the kingdom of God is to be found in Catholicism and no longer in Judaism. 9:2 **after six days.** This time frame connects the Transfiguration with the "seventh" day, the Lord's Day (Genesis 2:2-3). **Peter**... See the note on 3:16. **transfigured.** His appearance takes on a heavenly form. 9:3 **garments.** His garments show his glory (5:27; 6:56). 9:4 **Elijah with Moses.** Elijah represents the Prophets. Moses represents the Law. The Law and the Prophets make up the Old Testament, in which God prepared Israel for the Christ. This event shows that Jesus is the fulfillment of Judaism. Moses and Elijah were succeeded by Joshua and Elisha, respectively. Joshua and Elisha foreshadow Jesus' succession of Moses and Elijah, as the names "Joshua" and "Elisha" are forms of the name "Jesus." **talking to Jesus.** Their words are not given, but their talking together shows their union. **9:5 three booths.** The booths would be shelters for the three, and recall the Feast of Tabernacles (Leviticus 23:39-44). This may also reveal an expectation that Peter has that just as the Israelites lived in booths in the desert before they entered the Promised Land, perhaps now Jesus would lead them into (political?) liberation. He may also be underrating Jesus here by putting him on a level equal to Moses and Elijah, instead of recognizing Jesus' divinity. **9:6 he did not know...** Peter's offer to build booths is the only reverent thing he can think of to say. Fear keeps him from saying more (14:40). **9:7 cloud.** The cloud represents God (Exodus 16:10), especially the Holy Spirit. **voice...** See the note on 1:11. **my beloved Son.** The Father testifies that Jesus is the Son of God. See the note on 1:11. **listen to him.** Just as Jesus commanded obedience (8:33), so does God command it for Jesus. Jesus' words about suffering are not easy, but they are holy and need to be obeyed.

Jesus Teaches About Elijah (9:9-13)

9:9 until the Son of man... The secrecy command applies until the resurrection when the political dangers will have passed and the glory of God in Jesus must be proclaimed. See the note on 1:25. **9:10 questioning what...** They do not understand this because they cannot accept the fact that Jesus must suffer and die. **9:11 Elijah must come.** Malachi 4:5-6 prophesies that Elijah will return prior to the coming of the Christ. **9:12 how is it written...** Jesus contrasts the prophecy concerning Elijah's restoration of "all things" (Malachi 4:5-6) with prophecies concerning the Christ's suffering (Isaiah 52:13-53:12). The implication is that Elijah's mission will not have the permanent effects they expected. **9:13 Elijah has come.** There is no explicit identification of Elijah with John the Baptizer, but that is understood. See the note on 1:6. **as it is written...** John's martyrdom (6:14-29) reflects Jezebel's intentions towards Elijah (1 Kings 18:40; 19:2).

Jesus Casts Out the Dumb Demon (9:14-29)

9:14 scribes arguing... The scribes attack the disciples because they fail to cast out the demon. 9:15 greatly amazed. Jesus amazes the people like Moses did when his face glowed after a meeting with the Lord on a mountain (Exodus 34:29-30). 9:17 dumb spirit. A demon causes the boy to be mute. 9:18 it seizes him... The boy may have epilepsy. However, a medical explanation of his condition does not exclude a demon's involvement. 9:20 the spirit saw... Since this spirit is mute it will not call Jesus the Son of God (1:24, 34; 3:11; 5:7). Instead, the demon gives his testimony by showing power over the boy. 9:21 From childhood. The demon seems to have possessed the boy as long as the father has had a weak faith. 9:22 cast him into fire... Demons are obsessed with death (5:2, 13). if you can... The father's words reveal his low expectations. 9:23 If you can! The man's doubts offend Jesus. 9:24 I believe. The man repents of his lack of confidence and chooses to believe (1:15). Jesus grants faith to him who asks (James 1:5). 9:25 a crowd came... Jesus has separated himself (7:33; 8:23) from the crowd (9:14). deaf spirit. The casting out of a dumb and deaf spirit reminds us to speak God's praises and listen to Jesus' words. 9:26 crying out. See the note on 1:26. 9:27 Jesus took him... See the note on 1:31. 9:28 house. See the note on 1:29. 9:29 This kind. Jesus refers to the kind of demon that possesses someone who is under another's authority. The boy is under his father's authority. Parents' faith stands in place of their children's (5:21-24, 35-43; 7:24-30). prayer and fasting. The only prayer is the father's (9:24). Fasting is a form of repentance, and the father repents of his weak faith (9:24). Jesus casts out the demon because of the father's prayer and fasting.

Jesus' Second Prophecy of His Passion (9:30-32)

9:31 Son of man... This is the second prophecy of his death (8:31; 10:33). 9:32 afraid to ask. They remember Peter suffering a rebuke (8:32-33), and do not want another.

Jesus Teaches About Greatness (9:33-37)

9:33 house. Peter's house. See the note on 1:29. 9:34 on the way... See the note on 8:27. The disciples' musings on personal greatness contradict the way. 9:35 If any one would... Jesus does not rebuke the desire to be great; he redirects it. Greatness in God's eyes involves making oneself humble in the world's eyes. 9:36 child. Jesus points to a child, because serving a child does not make one appear great in the world's eyes. 9:37 receives one... Any person in need ought to be ministered to in Christ's name. To do so is to minister to Christ and even to God the Father. This applies especially to parents, as they must minister to their children.

He Who is Not Against Us is for Us (9:38-41)

9:38 man casting out... There is no indication of how this man received authority to cast out demons in Jesus' name (3:15; 6:7). not following us. The man is not one of the Twelve. 9:39 Do not forbid him. Jesus never rebukes true faith and its fruits (Numbers 11:26-29). 9:41 lose his reward. Faith in Jesus must be accompanied by works of Christian mercy. To avoid this is a sure way to lose God's kingdom.

Jesus Teaches Against Scandal (9:42-50)

9:42 Whoever causes... Jesus warns against scandal, the leading of another into sin. little ones. The little ones are anyone who could be led into sin. great millstone. This is a huge stone used to grind wheat into flour. Drowning is associated with condemnation to hell (see the note on 5:13; 11:23). 9:43, 45, 47 hand (foot, eye) causes. Sin comes from the mind's choosing, not from body parts (7:1-23). The body parts symbolize persons, places, or things that lead one to sin. These occasions of sin must be avoided, no matter how attached one is to them. The hand, foot, and eye are specified, as these are often used in sin. cut it off. Jesus is not teaching self-mutilation (Leviticus 19:28), but is emphasizing the extreme importance of cutting off one's own opportunities to sin. enter life. Jesus equates entering the kingdom of God (meaning Heaven) with "entering life." **hell.** Literally translated "Gehenna," a valley near Jerusalem used as a trash-burning site; it was once a place where children were sacrificed to pagan gods (2 Kings 23:10; Jeremiah 32:35). Jesus describes Hell in words his listeners can understand. **9:44, 46, 48 where their worm does not die, and the fire is not quenched.** These three identical verses quote Isaiah 66:24. They teach about the horrible, unending pains of Hell. Some ancient manuscripts do not have vv. 44, 46, and so most modern translations omit them. **9:49 salted with fire.** The fire is trials, temptations, and sufferings. Everyone endures these, so the difficult "cutting off" teaching is for everyone. **9:50 Salt is good...** If we give up our faith (lose saltiness), we lose the kingdom of God. We must have faith, and from faith comes peace with our fellow man. (See Leviticus 2:13.)

Unit VII

Jesus and Family Life

Introduction to Mark 10:1-52

Because of God's infinite love, the following is a story that God hates.

When the policeman arrived at the scene of the reported disturbance, he found the couple arguing about who got to keep the stereo. The wife was leaving and taking the TV, the VCR, and the stereo with her. The husband also wanted them. He was too angry to care that he was losing his wife. He hated her now.

The policeman helped resolve the dispute about the stuff, but he couldn't stop the death of a family.

Suddenly, the husband looked back at the house and saw their two young daughters in the doorway. The second custody battle wouldn't be as passionate as the first. He turned to his wife and bitterly asked, "Which one do you want?"

The wife paused, accepted the terms of this proposal, and said she wanted the older one. She called her. Her daughter came. They left.

Relieved that the battle was over and seeing his buddies across the street, he went to talk to them. Then he remembered his youngest daughter still standing in the doorway. Ignoring the fact that she had just lost her mother and her sister, he gruffly shouted at her to go to her room.

Their family life had died, and they all mourned alone.

God hates this story, because he loves each person in that family and he knows the pain they suffer.

Many of the things that happened in the story are condemned by Jesus in this section. Jesus condemns those things that damage people and estrange them from God.

But Jesus does not simply condemn. He shows us the way of God. And by his healings he shows us that he desires to heal the wounds we have inflicted.

In this story that God hates, we see a divorce in action. Jesus condemns divorce and shows the truth and beauty of marital unity.

In the story, we see a rejection of little children. Jesus embraces children and says the kingdom of God belongs to them and to those like them.

In the story, we see a greater love for riches than for God and others. We see a desire to be accepted by the world – in this case the man's buddies. We see a refusal to serve the one who is in need. Jesus addresses all these things here.

This section gives a diagnosis of the problems in many areas of our lives, including the family. It also gives the antidote. The Gospel is more about healing than condemnation. It is also about preventative medicine. Read on. The Doctor is waiting.

(For those who are divorced and remarried outside of the Church, it is strongly recommended that you learn the Church's compassionate teaching concerning your situation. The Church desires that you remain within the Church. Please see Pope John Paul II's Apostolic Exhortation, "*The Role of the Christian Family in the Modern World*", paragraphs 82-84.)

INDIVIDUAL STUDY
Read Mark 10:1-52 and then answer the following questions.

1. What did Moses permit if a man wanted a divorce?

2. What reason does Jesus give for forbidding divorce?

3. What does a person who remarries after divorce from a valid marriage commit?

4. How does Jesus initially respond to the man's question about obtaining eternal life?

5. What prevents the man from following Jesus' command to sell all he has?

6. What makes it hard for those with riches to enter the kingdom of God?

7. Does Jesus say that it is possible for men to be saved on their own?

8. Are Jesus' words about leaving family members an encouragement or a discouragement to the disciples?

9. What is most important in life?

10. Where are Jesus and the disciples going on the way?

11. What do James and John want from Jesus?

12. How should a follower of Jesus exercise authority?

13. What are two ways in which the sons of Zebedee and the son of Timaeus are similar?

14. What are two ways in which the sons of Zebedee and the son of Timaeus are different?

SHOP TALK:
Discuss these questions in your Bible study group.

GATHERING THE WOOD
(5 to 10 minutes)

● Begin with a prayer.

● Briefly describe your family's religious practices. How often do you attend Mass? How often does your family pray or discuss religious matters? What special customs does your family practice (e.g. at Christmas, Easter, Saints' Feast Days)?

BUILDING ON THE FOUNDATION (40 to 45 minutes)

Reread each passage before discussing it.

Marriage and Divorce (10:1-12)
Jesus' teaching was not easily accepted then, and it is not easily accepted now. But this is a wonderful teaching. What does it mean to you that a husband and wife become one flesh? What does it mean to you that God himself joins spouses together? What should young people preparing for marriage do to prevent divorce? What should married couples do to divorce-proof their marriage? What should someone who is in a marriage that took place outside the Church do?

Jesus Blesses the Children (10:13-16)
Jesus loves children. He embraces them and blesses them. If you have children in your home,

what can you do to bring them closer to Jesus? Why do you think this passage comes right after Jesus' teaching on marriage and divorce?

Money and Salvation (10:17-31)
The rich man's question is a marvelous one: he asks for the teaching we need. Jesus answers that obedience to God's commandments is absolutely necessary. Jesus goes on to teach that money and riches can take a person's heart away from God. What place should money have in a Christian's life?

The Request of James and John (10:35-45)
James and John want to be great. They desire to reign with Jesus in power. Jesus teaches them another way to be great. How can a leader be a servant? How can a servant be a leader?

The Request of Blind Bartimaeus (10:46-52)
Bartimaeus cries for help, and is rebuked by those who are annoyed by him. Jesus gives the blind man the attention he needs. When a person in your family annoys others, how can you improve the situation?

APPLYING THE FINISH
(10 minutes)

Mention one thing that you can do in your family to make it more Christian.

During the closing prayer, ask God, the source of all goodness, to give you the grace to be good to your family.

Explanations

Marriage and Divorce (10:1-12)

10:1 beyond the Jordan. Jesus goes to the Jordan River's eastern side, which was originally part of Israel (Joshua 22:1-9) and near where John the Baptizer ministered. **10:2 to test him.** The Pharisees test him by seeing if he will condemn divorce, which got John the Baptizer in trouble (6:14-29), or if Jesus will allow it, and so repudiate John. **10:4 Moses allowed...** Deuteronomy 24:1-4 regulated divorce in Israel, but did not establish it. **10:5 hardness of heart.** Had divorce not been permitted, many wives would have been killed so that their husbands could marry the women they wanted. The divorce certificate gave women legal protection. **10:6 God made them...** Jesus quotes Moses' writings to explain God's original intention. God's "making them male and female" (Genesis 1:27) implies that they are made for each other, and only for each other, thus excluding divorce and remarriage. **10:7 For this reason...** A man's leaving his parents is a separation from that natural bond and an entrance into a supernatural bond with his wife (Genesis 2:24). **10:8 one flesh.** Marriage, and particularly the marital act (sexual intercourse), unites spouses so that they become one body, one flesh. This union does not end when the marital act ends, but endures, so that the husband is part of his wife and vice versa. The bond is more than words and more than a physical act. They are united in their very beings. **10:9 God has joined...** The unity of marriage is not made by the spouses alone. God acts to make the two one. The Catholic Church does not allow divorce and remarriage because the Church does not

81

have the authority to overrule God. See *CCC* 1644-1651. **10:10 house.** See the note on 1:29. **10:11 commits adultery.** Adultery is committed by remarriage, because divorce does not end the marriage in God's eyes. The remarried man is still his first wife's husband. The remarried woman is still her first husband's wife.

Jesus Blesses the Children (10:13-16)

10:13 disciples rebuked them. The disciples consider Jesus' time too valuable to be spent with children. **10:14 to such belongs...** The children may not be able to have faith themselves, which is a requirement of the kingdom of God (1:15; 16:16), but the faith of their parents (who brought them to Jesus) covers them. **10:15 like a child.** The kingdom of God is a gift that is received, not earned. Children do nothing to earn the love of their parents. The children completely trust their parents to provide for them. Adults must receive the kingdom as a gift, and have complete trust in God's providence.

Money and Salvation (10:17-31)

10:17 knelt. Kneeling shows only partial obedience. The leper knelt before Jesus, but then disobeyed (1:40-45). Falling prostrate shows complete obedience (5:22, 33; 7:25). **what must I do...** The man's question focuses on actions, but he has faith that Jesus can show him what to do. **inherit.** Despite the needed actions, eternal life is still a gift that comes by a faith. The actions come from faith that lives. Actions preserve faith and thus preserve the "inheritance." See *CCC* 1987-2029. **10:18 Why do you...** Jesus offers the man an opportunity to recognize Jesus as God since Jesus is good and only God is good. **10:19 the commandments...** Jesus repeats the commandments that deal with love of neighbor (Exodus 20:12-17). Honoring parents is emphasized by placing it out of the normal order. **10:20 all these...** His words are a plea to know what he lacks, a plea that pleases Jesus. **10:21 loved him.** Jesus approves of his obedience. **You lack one thing...** The man serves both God and money, in violation of the commandment to love God alone (Exodus 20:2-6). A sacrifice is needed to commit his heart entirely to God. **come follow me.** The man is invited to join Jesus on the way. See the note on 8:27. **10:22 he went away...** The man values riches above eternal life (8:36). **10:24 amazed at his words.** The disciples see material blessings as evidence of God's favor. (Deuteronomy 28:1-14; Job 1:10; 42:10). **trust in riches.** It is not the possession of material goods but the trusting in them that is a problem. The temptation to trust riches increases the more one has. **10:25 It is easier...** A camel is the largest animal in Palestine. A needle's eye is a tiny opening. It is simply impossible for the camel to go through the needle's eye. A popular myth holds that one of Jerusalem's gates was called the eye of the needle. To enter it a camel was stripped of its baggage and went through on its knees. There is no evidence that any such gate ever existed. **10:26 who can be saved?** Everyone wants to be rich, and greed (excessive desire) is an obstacle to salvation. **10:27 it is impossible.** People simply cannot be saved apart from the power of God. **all things...** God gives people grace to overcome this desire and to overcome the attachment to possessions. **10:28 we have left...** Peter speaks truly (1:16-20). **10:29 house or brothers...** Jesus gives a list of riches that are often valued above God. **10:30 hundredfold now...** A hundredfold does not mean a 100% reward but 10,000%. The rewards for our sacrifices come now, as well as in Heaven where the rewards are even greater. **with persecutions.** The blessings on earth are accompanied by suffering. Suffering ends only in Heaven. **10:31 first will be last...** See 9:35.

Jesus' Third Prophecy of His Passion (10:32-34)

10:32 Jerusalem. The destination of his journey begun in 8:27 is now identified. **walking ahead...** Jesus shows his resolve to go to Jerusalem despite the power of his enemies. This amazes and frightens his disciples. **10:33-34 Son of man.** Jesus' third and final prophecy of his death and resurrection (8:31; 9:31).

The Request of James and John (10:35-45)

10:37 one at your right... Sitting at the hand of a king is a place of honor and power. They still seem to expect Jesus to establish his kingdom in a worldly way in Jerusalem. **10:38 the cup...** The cup symbolizes suffering. Baptism symbolizes martyrdom. **10:39 We are able.** James and John do not see the symbolism but only the symbols, and so answer affirmatively. **The cup that I...** Jesus prophesies the martyrdom of James and the severe torture of John. **10:40 those for whom...** Jesus will be crucified with two others, one on his right and one on his left (15:27). James and John are not thinking of being crucified. **10:42 who are supposed...** Leaders who spend time "lording" their power over others are not properly using authority. **10:44 slave of all.** Jesus uses the word "slave" to emphasize that authority is not for self-glorification, but entirely for the service of others, especially the weak. **10:45 Son of man...** Jesus is the model of authority, as he serves even the least ones. In his humanity he does not come as a king, but as a carpenter; not as a rich man, but as a poor one. **ransom for many.** His very life and death are for others. His death will be the ransom that frees people from their captivity to sin (Isaiah 53:10-12). Jesus does this for all – but not all accept this ransom.

The Request of Blind Bartimaeus (10:46-52)

10:46 Jericho. Jericho was the first city conquered by Joshua (Joshua 6:1-27). Here Jesus finds a man who will follow him on the way. See the note on 8:27. **Bartimaeus...** Bartimaeus means "son of Timaeus." All men are referred to in this way in addition to having a personal name (10:35). This is apparently his only name; he does not have a personal name. **10:47 Son of David.** The Christ is to be a descendant of King David (2 Samuel 7:12-13). This blind man sees that Jesus is the Christ. **10:48 cried out...** He shows persistent faith despite obstacles (13:13). **10:49 And they called...** The crowd shows a disturbing willingness to show kindness to a blind man when they know Jesus is looking, but rudeness when they think he isn't. **10:50 mantle.** The mantle symbolizes Bartimaeus' poverty, as it is his only possession (Exodus 22:26-27). In throwing it off, he does what the rich man could not (10:22). **10:51 What do you want...** The question is the same one posed to James and John (10:36). It is surprising because the answer seems obvious. **10:52 your faith...** Literally, the man's faith "saved" him. Faith brought him not only sight, but the kingdom of God. His faith is so great that he needs no special touches in order to be healed (8:22-26). There is no command to silence (see the note on 1:25). As Jesus is about to enter Jerusalem, he makes no effort to keep his messianic identity hidden. His crucifixion is inevitable. **on the way.** Bartimaeus follows Jesus on the way (see the note on 8:27).

Unit VIII
Bear Good Fruit

Introduction to Mark 11:1 - 12:44

On his way to violently stopping the Temple worship, Jesus curses a fig tree, causing it to wither to its roots. This seems to be the pointless destruction of a tree. Why does Jesus do this strange thing?

The answer begins with the tree itself. The tree bears no fruit. Mark informs us that it's not the season for bearing fruit. In order for it to do so now, it would need help from God.

The fig tree is a symbol of the Temple. Jesus comes to the Temple looking for fruit, but finds none. On its own, the Temple can bear no fruit. It must rely on God for help. Since it does not rely on God, it does not bear fruit.

Jesus curses the fig tree to explain what he is doing when he brings the Temple's sacrifices to a halt. Later he will prophesy that the Temple will wither (13:1-4).
But the fig tree does not just symbolize the Temple. It also symbolizes a person's life. If a person does not rely upon God and bear good fruit, then he meets the same fate as the cursed fig tree: he withers and dies.

The fig tree is a warning. It warns us of our need to produce good fruit.

Producing good fruit in our lives is like producing a good garden (see 4:26-29). It takes a lot of work to prepare the soil, plant the seeds, and do the fertilizing, watering, and weeding. But the gardener's work does not make the plant actually grow. The gardener simply makes the conditions for the plant's growth the best he can. The plant's actual growth is the work of God, performed through nature.

In our lives we prepare the soil of our souls. We remove the weeds of sin. We allow the seed of the Gospel to be planted in our lives. We water and fertilize the seed through prayer, Sacraments, morality, and fellowship with dedicated Christians. We labor over the conditions of our souls the best we can, but the actual growth of grace in us is not something we do. Rather, it is God's work in us. The fruit that comes from such a life delights the Lord and tastes sweet to us.

As you read this section, discover how Jesus teaches us to be fruitful.

INDIVIDUAL STUDY
Read Mark 11:1-12:44 and then answer the following questions.

1. What do the people do as Jesus rides into Jerusalem?

2. Why does Jesus curse the fig tree?

3. Which groups of people does Jesus prevent from doing their work?

4. What does Jesus say the Temple has become?

5. What two obstacles to effective prayer does Jesus point out?

6. Why do the chief priests and their company refuse to answer Jesus' question?

7. What happens to the son in the parable?

8. What should be rendered to Caesar, and why?

9. What should be rendered to God, and why?

10. Who does Jesus say will be the woman's husband in the resurrection, and why?

11. How should one love God?

12. Does Jesus deny that the Christ is the son of David?

13. What is it about the scribes that Jesus condemns?

14. How does the poor widow give more than the others?

Shop Talk:

Discuss these questions in your Bible study group.

Gathering the Wood

(5 to 10 minutes)

● Begin with a prayer.

● Briefly describe someone you know who is effective at what he does.

Building on the Foundation (40 to 45 minutes)

Reread each passage before discussing it.

Entering Jerusalem (11:1-11)

People singing Jesus' praises accompany his entrance into Jerusalem. Why are some people reluctant to sing or say the responses at Mass?

Jesus Stops the Temple Worship (11:15-19)

One reason Jesus stops the Temple sacrifices is because the Jews do not live their faith beyond the Temple. How are people tempted to live in ways contrary to the Faith?

Cursing the Fig Tree and Teaching About Prayer (11:12-14, 20-26)

Jesus curses the fig tree because, like the Temple, it yields no fruit. When Peter points out the withered tree, Jesus teaches about prayer. To be fruitful one must pray. What does Jesus say about prayer? How can you pray like that?

The Parable of the Tenants (12:1-12)

It seems the tenants rebel when the servants revealed that the tenants had produced no fruit. When the servants pointed this out, what should the tenants have done?

The Greatest Commandment (12:28-34)

Jesus declares that the love of God is the greatest commandment, and that the love of neighbor follows right behind. What does Jesus mean by love? Describe a person who truly loves God. Describe a person who truly loves his neighbor.

Jesus Condemns the Scribes (12:38-40)

Obviously the scribes do not produce good fruit. What would they need to change in order to do so?

The Contribution of the Poor Widow (12:41-44)

This widow gives to the Temple, where the scribes minister, and Jesus praises her for it. How does giving money to God bear good fruit? What should you do when those in charge of God's money are hypocrites? What about when they are virtuous?

Applying the Finish

(10 minutes)

Name one thing from this discussion that can make a difference in the fruitfulness of your life.

During the closing prayer, ask God to make your soul good soil that produces thirtyfold, sixtyfold, and a hundredfold (4:8).

Explanations

Entering Jerusalem (11:1-11)

11:1 Mount of Olives. The Lord is to appear on the Mount of Olives just before dividing Jerusalem (Zechariah 14:4). he sent two... See the note on 6:7. 11:2 colt. Jesus will fulfill Zechariah 9:9 as he enters Jerusalem. which no one... It is proper that an animal used in a liturgical event has never been used for labor. 11:3 The Lord has... The colt's owners will have faith in the Lord's words as presented through these apostles. 11:8 spread their garments... This is a sign of his being the king (2 Kings 9:13). They "roll out the red carpet" for him. 11:9 Hosanna! "Hosanna" is a word of praise to God for his gift of salvation. 11:10 kingdom of our father David. See the note on 10:47. 11:11 into the temple. This fulfills Malachi 3:1-2 (partially quoted in Mark 1:2). looked round. Jesus is looking for the Temple's fruit (11:13; 12:1-11).

Jesus Stops the Temple Worship (11:15-19)

11:15 drive out those... Jesus drives out everyone involved in the bringing of sacrifices to the altar, signaling the end of legitimate worship in the Temple. 11:17 My house. The Temple is God's dwelling on earth (1 Kings 8:4). for all nations. The business is transacted in the Temple area that is open to all peoples. den of robbers. This quote of Jeremiah 7:11 may refer to unfair business practices; however, robbers typically do not rob in their dens. The Jews are robbers in that they live one way in the Temple and another way outside of it, thus robbing God of the glory he should be given in their daily lives (see Jeremiah 7:1-34). The Temple has sadly become the gathering place, the den, for these robbers. **11:18 sought a way...** This is the second plotting of Jesus' death (3:6; 14:1).

Cursing the Fig Tree (11:12-14)

11:13 fig tree in leaf. Fig trees get leaves in early Spring (which is the time of this event, the time just before the Passover), but do not produce figs until June. It would take a work of God to make a fig tree fruitful so early. **11:14 May no one...** The fig tree is a symbol of the Temple. Jesus pronounces a curse not just on the tree but on the Temple, because of its unfruitfulness (Jeremiah 8:13).

Teaching About Prayer (11:20-26)

11:20 withered away... Fig trees have a lot of sap. For a leafy fig tree to wither to the roots this quickly would take a miracle. **11:22 Have faith in God.** The Temple is cursed (see the note on 11:14) because of its faithlessness. **11:23 this mountain.** An apparent reference to the Temple mountain. **cast into the sea.** Drowning in the sea signifies condemnation (5:13; 9:42). **does not doubt.** God answers prayers that show trust, not ones that show doubt (9:23). **11:24 it will be yours.** This is not about making God a slave to people. People are called to have faith in God, which means they must put his will before their own. God desires to provide for our every need (but not our every luxury). **11:25 forgive.** Prayer begins with reconciliation with God and others. **11:26 But if you do not forgive, neither will your Father who is in heaven forgive your trespasses.** This verse is missing from some ancient manuscripts and so is left out of most modern translations. It duplicates Matthew 6:15. Refusing to forgive others results in God refusing to forgive us and hear our prayers.

The Conflict over Jesus' Authority (11:27-33)

11:27 walking in the temple. This walking and the conversation that follows implies that Jesus continues his prophetic act of the day before, as he goes about the Temple preventing any more sacrifices (11:15-16). 11:28 By what authority. The chief priests are the Temple authorities. They deem Jesus' actions to be a rebellion against them and God. 11:31 argued... They do not debate the truth of the matter, but the political consequences of their response. 11:33 Neither will I... By saying this, Jesus implies that John's authority has the same origin as his own.

The Parable of the Tenants (12:1-12)

12:1 parables. See the note on 4:2. A man. God. vineyard. Israel. set a hedge... God provided everything Israel needed to bear good fruit. tenants. God established authorities to govern Israel and lead it to be holy. another country. God is not tangibly present to Israel. 12:2 servant. The servants are the holy men of the Old Testament. 12:3 empty-handed. The tenants have failed to produce fruit and violently hate the servant for requesting it. 12:6 beloved. See the note on 1:11. They will respect... This refers to how the son ought to be treated, not how he will be treated. 12:7 let us kill him. See Genesis 37:12-36. inheritance... The tenants, the Jewish leaders, want power over others more than they want to please God. 12:9 He will come... The Temple and these Jewish leaders will be destroyed in 70 A.D. (see Isaiah 5:1-7), and the Church will have already become the Lord's new vineyard. 12:10-11 The very stone... Jesus quotes Psalm 118:22-23 to say that he is the stone that is the foundation for the Lord's Church. 12:12 they perceived... This is the only time anyone is said to grasp a parable's meaning (4:10-12, 33-34).

The Conflict over Taxes (12:13-17)

12:14 Is it lawful... Paying taxes to the Roman Empire means using coins that bore images of Caesar and referred to him as a god, both violations of the Mosaic Law (Exodus 20:2-4). Also, it is a recognition of a non-Jewish authority over them, which is "unacceptable." The Christ is expected to overthrow such authorities, not advise paying taxes to them. Therefore, Jesus will look "unChrist-like" if he says "Pay the taxes." If he says "Do not pay", then he is a rebel who the Herodians would put to death (see the note on 3:6). **12:15 Bring me a coin.** Jesus does not have such a coin, but they do. **12:17 Render to Caesar.** Since the coin bears Caesar's image, it belongs to Caesar, and should be given back to him. **Render to God.** Humans bear God's image (Genesis 1:27) and belong to him. Jesus calls them to conversion (1:15).

The Conflict over the Resurrection (12:18-27)

12:18 Sadducees. The Sadducees are a religious party that judged the five Mosaic books (Genesis, Exodus, Leviticus, Numbers, and Deuteronomy) alone to be inspired Scripture. **no resurrection.** They deny that there is life after death. **12:19 if a man's brother...** See Deuteronomy 25:5-10. **12:25 neither marry.** Death ends a marriage. **like angels.** Angels do not beget new angels. In heaven, marriage is unnecessary as there is no begetting of new children. **12:26 about the bush.** See Exodus 3:6. This phrase points to the resurrection. The bush was on fire but did not burn up. The expectation was that fire would consume the bush, but the power of God saved it. With death, the expectation is that death would consume the body, but the power of God will raise the body at the resurrection. **12:27 not God of the dead...** God stated that he is *presently* God of Abraham, Isaac, and Jacob (all of whom had long since died). He did not say he *was* their God. This means they are alive by the power of God.

The Greatest Commandment (12:28-34)

12:28 Which commandment... There are 613 commandments in Judaism; this question is an understandable one. **12:29-30 Hear, O Israel...** Jesus quotes Deuteronomy 6:4-5. God alone is God. He alone is to be loved as God. We must love him with our whole beings. Jesus adds "with all your mind" to the quote, which helps explain "with all your soul". **12:31 The**

second. Jesus adds to his answer by giving the second commandment, Leviticus 19:18. The second is lower than the first, but inextricably connected to it. **12:33 all whole burnt...** The scribe recognizes that love of God, not external acts, is the foundation of true religion. **12:34 not far...** Jesus does not declare the scribe to be in the kingdom of God, apparently because he has not yet come to actual faith in Jesus.

The Conflict over the Son of David (12:35-37)

12:35 How can... Jesus points out a seeming contradiction in order to lead the people to a deeper understanding of the Christ. He thus gives an example for us to follow when we come across seeming contradictions in Scripture. **Christ is...** Jesus has already accepted both of these titles (8:29; 10:47-48). **12:36 David himself, inspired...** Jesus testifies to the divine authorship of Scripture. **The Lord said...** Jesus quotes Psalm 110:1. The first "Lord" is the Lord God. The second is the Christ, David's son. Calling one's own son "Lord" is wholly inappropriate. The Christ must be more than David's son, even though he is David's son. Jesus wants the people to see that the Christ is the Son of God. **till I put...** Victory over his enemies (the scribes, Pharisees, etc.) is promised to Jesus. **12:37 great throng...** The crowd takes delight in the scribes being humbled – but Herod also gladly heard John the Baptizer before ordering his death (6:20).

Jesus Condemns the Scribes (12:38-40)

12:38 long robes. Exceptionally long robes are supposed to symbolize exceptional devotion to God. **12:40 devour widow's houses.** Widows need legal protection after their spouses' death. Scribes give them that protection, but at an unfair price. Then the scribes cover their evil actions with pious acts. **condemnation.** God vows revenge against those who oppress widows (Exodus 22:21-23).

The Contribution of the Poor Widow (12:41-44)

12:41 sat down opposite. This is a position of judgment (13:3; 15:39). Jesus sits in judgment while the people make their contributions. **12:42 poor widow.** It is implied that the widow is poor because of the scribes (12:40). **two copper coins.** She could decide to keep one. **12:44 out of their abundance.** Others give what they do not need. Their gifts are not worth much to them. The widow gives from what she needs, showing her child-like reliance on God to provide for her (10:15). True love gives until it hurts.

Unit IX
The Coming of the Son of Man

Introduction to Mark 13:1-37

"You mean Jesus is coming back?" Monica asked.

"Yes," said her mother. "At the end of the world, Jesus will come back to earth, and the whole world will see him at once."

Monica was in awe. All her short life she had learned about Jesus, but somehow she had missed the fact that Jesus would return. This truly amazed her.

Her mother saw the wonder in her eyes, and began to realize how much she herself had taken Jesus' Second Coming for granted.

What a truly glorious event that will be! No one knows when it will happen. We simply know that it will. And although we rarely talk about it, our curiosity leads us to hope to see it happen.

Although the primary meaning of this chapter is about the destruction of the Jerusalem Temple, the secondary meaning is about the Second Coming of Jesus. When he speaks of the trials and the sufferings that will occur before the Temple's destruction, we know he's also referring to later trials and sufferings.

Jesus tells us all these things so that, when tribulations come, we will know that he stands on the other side of them, waiting to gather us in and save us. This will help those who do live in the End Times, but it also helps every generation of Christians because every single person experiences suffering in this life. All Christians are tempted to give up the battle and be untrue to Jesus. So Jesus teaches us that he who perseveres to the end will be saved. There is suffering, but there's something to hope for, too.

When the destruction of the Jerusalem Temple happened in 70 A.D., something remarkable did not happen then: the death of any Christian. The Christians saw what was about to take place and remembered Jesus' words to flee Jerusalem when they saw the signs Jesus gives here. They were not killed like so many thousands of Jews were, because they had vacated the entire region. God had led his people away from that danger. The Christians suffered greatly when they left Jerusalem, but God rewarded their obedience.

Pray much when you read this section. Jesus' words may be hard to understand, but they are worth understanding. (Be sure to make use of the "Explanations" to get the most out of the material.)

INDIVIDUAL STUDY

Read Mark 13:1-37 and then answer the following questions.

1. Upon hearing the Temple praised for its beauty, what does Jesus say will happen to it?

2. Who comes to ask Jesus about the timing of the Temple's destruction?

3. What is the first sign that the Temple will be destroyed?

4. What is the second sign that the Temple will be destroyed?

5. What is the third sign that the Temple will be destroyed?

6. What should the follower of Jesus say when he is put on trial?

7. Who will be saved?

8. What is the fourth sign that the Temple will be destroyed?

9. What is the fifth sign that the Temple will be destroyed?

10. What is the sixth sign that the Temple will be destroyed?

11. What are the events that will happen when the Son of man appears, coming in the clouds?

12. Who alone knows when the Son of man will return?

13. In this final parable, what does Jesus command of his followers?

14. What does Jesus warn his followers against in the final parable?

SHOP TALK:

Discuss these questions in your Bible study group.

GATHERING THE WOOD

(5 to 10 minutes)

- Begin with a prayer.

- Perseverance pays off. Briefly describe how you worked on something for a long time and finally accomplished your goal.

BUILDING ON THE FOUNDATION (40 to 45 minutes)

Reread each passage before discussing it.

Persevere During Trials (13:1-13)

Jesus speaks of terrible trials for Christians as they bring the Gospel to others. He tells of being hated by all, including family members, for the sake of the Gospel. How should you respond when a family member rejects you because you are living the Christian faith?

The Tribulation (13:14-23)

Jesus describes the destruction of the Temple. His words also refer to the tribulation that will come before the end of the world. Those times will certainly be difficult, but he reminds us of our hope when he says, "But he who endures to the end will be saved" (13:13). The Temple has already been destroyed. The end of the world is yet to come. Regardless of whether or not the end of the world will happen in our lifetimes, the message of perseverance still applies. How difficult is it to persevere in faith right now? How would the tribulation described by Jesus make it hard to persevere? When times are tough, what can help you stand fast?

The Second Coming (13:24-27)

Jesus did not tell us when he would return, but he did warn us to always be ready for him. What happens to those who are ready for his return? What happens to those who are not ready? What can you do to help people be ready?

Be Prepared (13:28-37)

Jesus has promised us that he will return. It is not a matter of "if" but "when," although Jesus teaches here that it is absolutely foolish to try to determine when that will be. What does Jesus say should be done in order to be ready for his return? What do you need to do to meet Jesus' standards?

APPLYING THE FINISH

(10 minutes)

If you get many more years to persevere in the faith, what will your life look like in the time just before you die?

During the closing prayer, ask Jesus to help you persevere in times of trouble.

Explanations

Persevere During Trials (13:1-13)

13:2 thrown down. The Temple had been destroyed in 587 B.C. by the Babylonians, and this was understood as a sign that God was angry with his people's infidelity (2 Kings 25:8-17). The Temple's destruction by the Romans that Jesus prophesizes here will take place in 70 A.D. **13:3 opposite the temple.** Jesus is in a position of judgment (12:41; 15:39). **Peter and...** These four disciples have been with Jesus from the beginning (1:16-20), and now they will learn about the End (13:24-28). **13:5 Jesus began to say.** 13:1-37 is concerned primarily with the Temple's destruction, but it also refers to the "End Times" in a secondary way. In the Old Testament, the Temple is understood as a miniature model of the universe. As the Temple is the place of God's dwelling during the Old Testament, the universe becomes the place of God's dwelling through the Incarnation in the New Testament. The judgment of God visited on the Temple and the judgment of God on the universe are two sides of the same event. Therefore, Jesus' words about the Temple here also apply to the End of the Universe. **13:6 in my name.** This contrasts with the disciples' encounter with a strange exorcist (9:38-39). The difference is that the dangerous one is more concerned with drawing people to himself than with leading them to Jesus. **I am he!** The false ones will claim to be Christs. **13:7 the end.** The Temple's end and also the world's end. **13:8 nation will rise...** Jesus speaks of both man-made and natural catastrophes. **the beginning...** The signs come before the event, but there may be a long while before the event actually takes place. The message is "be prepared always." **13:9 they will deliver...**

What Jesus prophesies will happen to his followers (13:9, 11-13) are things he himself will go through (14:10-15:37). **bear testimony.** This involves a willingness to die for the Gospel. **13:10 gospel must first...** This happened before the Temple's destruction in 70 A.D., insofar as the Gospel was preached to all the nations of the Roman Empire, the known world at the time. **13:11 say whatever is given...** He who trusts in God will be inspired by God (12:36; Exodus 4:10-12). **13:12 brother will deliver...** Jesus experienced rejection by relatives (3:21; 6:4) and will be delivered up by his "brother" Judas (14:43). **13:13 hated by all.** Jesus is abandoned by all at his crucifixion (15:27-34). **he who endures...** Jesus interrupts the announcement of martyrdoms with a message of hope. Salvation comes to the one who never gives up (2:1-12; 5:21-43; 7:24-30; 10:46-52; 14:3-9).

The Tribulation (13:14-23)

13:14 desolating sacrilege... This sacrilege will desecrate the Temple. Christians should flee when they see that this sacrilege will soon occur. They should not wait for it to happen. **where it ought.** The Greek has "he, not "it," suggesting the sacrilege is a person or persons (Luke 21:20). **let the reader understand.** Jesus points the disciples back to Scripture, to see the desolating sacrilege of the past as a forerunner of the new one. The past sacrilege was the establishment of a statue of Zeus in the Temple by Greek forces (Daniel 11:31; 1 Maccabees 1:54-58; 2 Maccabees 6:1-5). This one will be the attack and destruction of Jerusalem by the pagan Roman army. **in Judea.** All Christians in the region should flee from Jerusalem. **13:15 let him who is...** The destruction will be so severe that material possessions must be left behind (8:35-38; 10:23-31, 42-44). **13:17 Alas for those...** Flight will be most difficult for those who have dependents. Jesus is not discouraging having children. **13:18 Pray that...** Prayer is powerful (11:21-26). God's mercy desires to lessen the tribulation's severity, but his justice demands that it take place. **13:19 For in those days...** "(T)he sufferings of the people were so fearful that they can hardly be told, and no other city ever endured such miseries. Not since the world began was there a generation more prolific in crime than this bastard scum [the Jews leading the revolt against the Romans] of the nation who destroyed the city" (Josephus, a first century Jewish historian who sided with the Romans and witnessed the destruction of Jerusalem. Quote taken from "The

Jewish War," translated by Paul L. Maier in *Josephus: The Essential Writings*, p.347, Kregel Publications: Grand Rapids, Michigan, 1988.) **13:20 shortened the days.** During the tribulation the Lord shortens the number of days, not the length of each day. **no human...** The tribulation will be so severe that no one could endure to the end without the mercy of God. **13:22 False Christs...** There is always the danger of false religious leaders arising, stating they know when or where the Christ is returning, or even claiming to be the Christ. **signs and wonders.** Jesus performs signs so that the people repent and believe (1:15). He refuses to work miracles to merely impress or entertain people (8:11-12). The false one's signs will not come from God. **to lead astray, if possible...** The elect are those chosen by God, who accept God's choosing them. Christians will leave Christ for false Christs, but the elect will not give in to this temptation.

The Second Coming (13:24-27)

13:24 sun will be darkened... The heavenly lights are prevented from doing what characterizes them; the sun and moon give off no light. The fixed stars fall. These things are not a sign of the Second Coming – they happen because of it. These heavenly bodies refer to elements of the Temple as well as extraordinary signs in the universe. **13:26 they.** Jesus said "you" when referring to the desolating sacrilege (13:14). Saying "they" now means that this event is not one that Jesus' followers will witness as they will have abandoned Jerusalem. **Son of man.** See the note on 2:10. Jesus uses this title to emphasize that the divine being who comes in glory is the same divine Person that stands before them in the flesh. The judgment on the Temple is, in a certain sense, a coming of the Son of man. **13:27 send out the angels...** Jesus sends out the angels as he sends the disciples (6:7; 16:15). See the note on 1:13. On one hand, this points to the salvation of all of God's people. On the other hand, it points to the strengthening of Christians everywhere in the interim between the end of the Temple and the end of the world.

Be Prepared (13:28-37)

13:28 fig tree. A fig tree's annual cycle is so regular that a man can tell the time of year by its appearance. This recalls the cursed fig tree (11:12-14, 20-

21). **13:29 he is near...** This "he" refers to the desolating sacrilege (13:14), not the Son of man (13:26). The reference to the gates indicates Jesus is speaking about Jerusalem, a walled city that is entered through a few different gates. **13:30 this generation...** "This generation" comprises the people alive at that time (8:12, 38; 9:19). The Temple's destruction will be less than 40 years after Jesus' Ascension. **13:31 Heaven and earth...** Jesus emphasizes the certainty of his prophecy with these words. He means that not only will the Temple be destroyed – it will never be rebuilt. The rebuilding of the Temple would mean that Jesus' words have passed away. The Temple has never been rebuilt. **13:32 But of that day...** Jesus is not saying that the Son of God doesn't know the time of the Temple's destruction or of the Second Coming at the End of the world. Rather, his words mean that Jesus has in no way revealed when that shall be. It is absolutely futile to study Scripture, the written revelation of Jesus Christ, to try to determine the timing of his return. **13:33 watch and pray.** This is the mission Jesus gives: watch for the signs and be in union with God through prayer. In this way, his followers will be prepared whenever Jesus comes. **13:34 a man going...** See the notes on 12:1-11. This time Jesus is the man who goes away. He leaves his followers in charge of his house, the Church. (See the note on 1:29.) Each person in the Church has a task to carry out in the waiting period before the Second Coming. The doorkeeper symbolizes each Christian, as each Christian must be on watch. **13:35 in the evening...** These are the four watches of the night. Jesus' disciples will fail at each watch: in the evening (14:32-42), at midnight (14:43-52), at cockcrow (14:66-72), and in the morning (15:1-15). **13:37 I say to all: Watch.** Even if one does not live in the End Times, all must die and face Judgment. So we all must be prepared.

Unit X

Betrayal

Introduction to Mark 14:1-72

Saint Joseph was the first person to have a chance to put Jesus to death.

While Joseph was betrothed to Mary, but before they lived together, he learned that Mary was pregnant. He knew he wasn't the father (see Matthew 1:18-24).

The Law of Moses allowed Joseph to have Mary put to death (Deuteronomy 22:23-24), since the natural assumption would be that Mary must have had relations with another man.

Under the Law, Mary would have been put to death by stoning. Since she was pregnant, her child, Jesus, would die as well.

Joseph could have easily concluded that another man had taken his wife-to-be for his own pleasure. He could have easily concluded that he had been betrayed.

Yet he was unwilling to put Mary and her child to death. He considered sending her away, in order to avoid putting her and her child to public shame.

Instead of focusing on the possibility of his being betrayed, Joseph focused on the needs of others, specifically, the needs of Mary and the Christ Child. Instead of giving in to the temptation of anger, he looked for what was best for Mary and Jesus. Perhaps he knew that Mary was innocent and considered sending her away because he thought himself unworthy to protect Mary and Jesus.

In any case, Joseph chose to save, not condemn.

Jesus came to forgive sins (2:10) and ransom people out of sin (10:45). He did so as God, certainly, but he had a great earthly role model in St. Joseph, the man who decided not to condemn Jesus to death despite what looked like a terrible sin.

Eventually, an angel appeared to Joseph and eased his anxiety. The Lord wanted Joseph to raise the child as his own.

Still, Joseph could have refused the angel's request. Refusal must have been tempting. He knew people would whisper because of the early pregnancy and the appearance of immorality. He knew taking this on meant the end of any ambitions to worldly greatness he might have had. He chose loyalty to God and Christ. He knew, no matter who opposed him and no matter what danger threatened him, that God supported him.

In this section you will read about the unfaithfulness of many men to Jesus, and the great faithfulness of Jesus to God and to us. Those who are loyal and those who are disloyal should both inspire us to greater loyalty to Jesus Christ.

INDIVIDUAL STUDY

Read Mark 14:1-72 and then answer the following questions.

1. Why do the chief priests and scribes want to arrest Jesus by stealth?

2. What does the woman in Bethany do to Jesus?

3. Why does Jesus praise her action?

4. What does Jesus teach his disciples about the betrayer?

5. What does Jesus do with the cup?

6. What does Jesus prophesy concerning his disciples?

7. What does Peter boast to Jesus?

8. Who is closest to Jesus when he goes to pray?

9. What does Jesus command his disciples to do in Gethsemane?

10. What does Jesus say in his prayer?

11. What happens to Jesus' followers after his arrest?

12. How many questions does the high priest ask Jesus?

13. How does the high priest react to Jesus' admission that he is the Christ, the Son of God?

14. How many times is Peter accused of being a follower of Jesus?

SHOP TALK:

Discuss these questions in your Bible study group.

GATHERING THE WOOD

(5 to 10 minutes)

● Begin with a prayer.

● Briefly describe a friend who was loyal to you when it was not easy to be so.

BUILDING ON THE FOUNDATION (40 to 45 minutes)

Reread each passage before discussing it.

The Woman with the Costly Nard (14:3-9)

This woman's love for Jesus inspires a great sacrifice for him. But some get angry with her. Would you have approved or disapproved of her actions? If your parish wanted to build an expensive new church, what would your reaction be?

Jesus Announces the Betrayal (14:17-21)

The betrayer is so intimate with Jesus that he "dips bread in the dish" with him. In a sense, receiving Communion is "dipping bread in the dish" with Jesus. How do you prepare yourself to receive Communion so that you receive worthily?

Jesus Institutes the Eucharist (14:22-25)

Jesus gives his disciples his Body and Blood. This is a sign of Jesus' loyalty to his Father and to us. What does Jesus' gift of the Eucharist mean to you?

Jesus Announces the Abandonment (14:26-31)

The disciples promise loyalty as their emotions in-spire them. But fear will inspire their betrayal. How can someone become stronger than his emotions?

Jesus' Prayer of Submission (14:32-42)

Jesus sees how difficult loyalty to the Father will be, but in his prayer he chooses loyalty anyway. By not praying, the disciples fail to be loyal. Describe a time when you prayed and God helped you to be loyal to him.

Betrayal and Abandonment of Jesus (14:43-52)

When Jesus is arrested, what could happen to a disciple who remained loyal?

Jesus' Trial Before the High Priest (14:53-65)

Look at how Jesus responds to the lies and the physical attack. In what kind of situations should you imitate this?

Peter's Trial Before the High Priest's Maid (14:66-72)

Jesus admits who he is before the High Priest. Peter denies who he is before a lowly maid. What does this say about Jesus? About Peter?

APPLYING THE FINISH

(10 minutes)

By the Sacrament of Reconciliation, God forgives Catholics of disloyalty to the Lord and his Church. State one thing you appreciate about this Sacrament.

During the closing prayer, thank Jesus for being true and loyal.

Explanations

Plotting of Jesus' Death (14:1-2)

14:1 two days before... The Passover and Unleavened Bread celebrations annually remind Israel of God's freeing them from slavery in Egypt (Exodus 12:1-51; 34:18). chief priests... This is the third plotting of Jesus' death (3:6; 11:18).

The Woman with the Costly Nard (14:3-9)

14:3 house of Simon... See the note on 1:29. That this Simon is called a leper emphasizes Jesus' love for the poor (9:35-37; 10:14). poured it... This recalls the anointing of the kings of Israel (1 Samuel 10:1) and the anointing of the Holy Spirit at his baptism (1:10). 14:4 there were some... No one complained when the widow gave her two coins (12:41-44). 14:5 three hundred denarii. About a year's wages. 14:7 For you always... By praising her act, Jesus emphasizes the need to love God before loving neighbor (12:28-34). 14:8 anointed my body... Jewish custom requires that a corpse be anointed before burial (16:1). This anointing prepares for his death. 14:9 wherever the gospel... The woman's sacrifice earns her a reward from God (Proverbs 19:17).

Judas' Betrayal (14:10-11)

14:11 promised to give him money. This is the only motive mentioned for betraying Jesus.

Passover Preparations (14:12-16)

14:12 first day of Unleavened Bread. The actual first day of Unleavened Bread begins the day after Passover (Leviticus 23:5-6). Because the two feasts are connected, Passover is sometimes called the first day of Unleavened Bread (2 Chronicles 35:17). The reference to bread recalls the theme of bread in 6:6-8:21. **14:13 he sent two.** See the notes on 11:1. **a man carrying...** This man recalls John, who prepared the way for Jesus with baptismal water (1:2-11).

Jesus Announces the Betrayal (14:17-21)

14:20 dipping bread... Eating together shows trust. Judas' betrayal breaks that trust (Psalm 41:9). **14:21 as it is written...** For example, see Isaiah 52:13-53:12. **It would have...** This may refer to a punishment in Hell (9:42-48), but it certainly refers to the evil of the betrayal.

Jesus Institutes the Eucharist (14:22-25)

14:22 took bread... Blessing the bread (6:41; 8:6) invests it with holiness. Breaking the bread foreshadows his sufferings. **this is my body.** This bread is his body because Jesus said so. Even when they seem impossible, Jesus' words always prove true (2:8-12; 5:39; 7:29-30; 11:1-6; 14:12-16). Within the Passover celebration, which was part of God's plan to liberate the Israelites from death and slavery (Exodus 12:1-13), an unblemished male lamb was sacrificed and eaten by the Israelites. Jesus is the new Passover lamb. Eating his body is the way of salvation. See *CCC* 1333-1344. **14:23 cup.** Wine is drunk at Passover meals. **given thanks.** "Eucharist" comes from the Greek for "giving thanks." **14:24 This is my blood...** The Mosaic Law calls for animal blood to atone for sins (Leviticus 4:1-35). Christ's blood will atone for all sins. **covenant.** Blood is used to make a covenant (Exodus 23:3-8, 11). Jesus' blood seals a new covenant (Jeremiah 31:31-34). In a covenant God makes a bond with his people, making them his family. Sin ruptured the old covenant, so Jesus makes a new one in order to destroy sin and restore (and perfect) the sacred family bond with God. Jesus' body and blood become the covenant meal through which we deepen our union with God. **poured out for many.** This Eucharist is the fulfillment of Jesus' prophecy in 10:45. **14:25 I shall not drink...** This means his suffering and death are about to begin. Jesus never speaks of his death without referring to his resurrection (8:31; 9:31; 10:33). Drinking the wine "new in the kingdom of God" refers to his resurrection victory over sin and death, and the true celebration that is Heaven.

Jesus Announces the Abandonment (14:26-31)

14:26 sung a hymn. The Passover ritual ends with Psalm 118, which thanks God for the Savior. **14:27 it is written...** Jesus quotes Zechariah 13:7. **14:28 Galilee.** See the note on 16:7. **14:30 this very night...** True loyalty is about more than feelings. **the cock crows.** The cock crows at sunrise.

Jesus' Prayer of Submission (14:32-42)

14:33 Peter... Jesus pulls aside his most intimate disciples (3:16; 5:37; 9:2) for his most difficult prayer. **14:34 watch.** Watching implies praying (13:33). **14:35 a little farther.** Jesus wants his disciples near him, but he ultimately makes his prayer alone. **fell on the ground.** Prostration shows total submission (5:22, 33; 7:25). **the hour might...** The hour is the time of Jesus' suffering and death. **14:36 Abba, Father.** "Abba" is Aramaic for "Father." It expresses the intimate relationship Jesus has with God the Father. **all things...** God could save us in another way, but he chooses the way of the cross. **remove this cup.** The cup of suffering (10:38-39; 14:23-24). **not what I will...** Jesus is fully human, and human nature avoids suffering and death. Jesus' divinity does not prevent that. He completely submits his human will to the Father's. **14:37 Simon.** Jesus calls Peter by his original name (1:16), showing that he is failing to follow Jesus' call. Peter alone is spoken to; he is the disciple Jesus places closest to himself. **14:38 Watch and pray...** Jesus repeats his command (14:34) and warns that failure to obey will lead to failure in their impending trial. **the spirit is willing...** Jesus wants them to rely on God's strength, not their own. **14:40 they did not know...** They have no excuse, despite their weak flesh (9:6). **14:41 the third time...** Jesus' prayer and movements are described less and less. The failure to pray results in Jesus' fading away from them. **It is enough.** The time of praying and of sleeping is over because, the trial is at hand. **the hands of sinners.** They sin by arresting him.

Betrayal and Abandonment of Jesus (14:43-52)

14:43 one of the twelve. Judas' intimacy with Jesus is emphasized (3:19; 14:10) as he betrays Jesus. **14:44 a sign.** Darkness and the fact that not everyone has seen Jesus make a sign necessary. **under guard.** Judas rightly expects some resistance (14:47). **14:46 laid hands on him.** This fulfills Jesus' words (9:33; 14:41). **14:47 drew his sword...** An unnamed disciple (but see John 18:10) attempts an act of righteousness (Numbers 25:7-8), but the resistance ends quickly, as it does not reflect Jesus' submission to the arrest. **slave of the high priest.** This implicates the high priest in the betrayal. **his ear.** This signifies the mob's deafness to Jesus' words (4:9, 12; 8:18). **14:48 Have you come...** Jesus challenges them to decide who they believe him to be. They choose to treat him as a criminal. **14:49 Day after day...** Jesus challenges their motive in arresting him at night, giving them a chance to repent. They are unwilling to let their deeds be done in the light. **let the scriptures...** Jesus refers to Isaiah 53:7, 12 and Zechariah 13:7. **14:50 they all...** Jesus' prophecy in 14:27 is fulfilled. **14:51-52 young man...** This young man may be Mark. This would then be Mark's way of saying that his only contribution to Jesus' earthly ministry was to abandon him. **left the linen cloth...** The linen cloth symbolizes unity with Jesus (5:15). Leaving it shows the disciples' abandonment. Unity will be restored, however (15:46; 16:5).

Jesus' Trial Before the High Priest (14:53-65)

14:53 they led Jesus... This is the climax of all the plottings (3:6; 11:18; 14:1-2, 10-11). 14:54 by the fire. May also be translated "by the light". Peter is about to be exposed (14:66-72). 14:55 put him to death. The trial's purpose is not justice, but to find a way to execute him. 14:56 many bore false... By lying, the witnesses break the Mosaic Law (Exodus 20:16). Their testimonies are insufficient, because at least two witnesses must agree in order to find someone guilty of a capital crime (Numbers 35:30). 14:58 I will destroy... There is no saying of Jesus like this in Mark (but see John 2:19). The saying of Jesus that is contorted here refers to the temple of his body being destroyed and raised on the third day. The accusation reflects a tradition, based on 2 Samuel 7:13, that held that the Christ would build a new Temple. Thus they accuse Jesus of wanting to destroy the Temple and of claiming to be the Christ. These accusations reappear when Jesus is on the cross (15:29-32), but he will be vindicated upon his death (15:38-39). made with hands. This phrase means they accuse Jesus of calling the Temple an idol (Psalm 115:4). 14:60 the high priest... The frustrated high priest tries to get Jesus to incriminate himself. The high priest's questions show that Jesus was silent during the false testimonies (15:4). 14:61 Are you the Christ... Finally, the true identity of Jesus (1:1) appears on the lips of a mortal man. However, it comes as an accusation, not a confession. "Blessed" is another word for "God" here. The high priest hypocritically uses another word for God to show reverence to him, while he condemns the Son of God. 14:62 I am. Jesus confesses his true identity using the divine name (see the note on 6:50). you will see... Jesus combines Daniel 7:13 and Psalm 110:1. Jesus will come seated on the Throne of God (8:38; 12:35-37; 13:24-27). "Power" is another word for God here. Jesus shows true reverence and true justice when he uses another word for God. The high priest will see this event at his judgment (and at the Temple's destruction). The world will see it at the Second Coming. 14:63 high priest tore... Tearing garments is a sign of offense at hearing blasphemy (Joshua 7:6). The high priest is not supposed to rend his garments (Leviticus 21:10). This dissolves the Jewish high priesthood (see the note on 15:38). 14:64 his blasphemy. Jesus spoke the truth, but the high priest calls it blasphemy (Leviticus 24:16). 14:65 cover his face... A popular understanding of Isaiah 11:2-4 held that the Christ could learn the truth simply by his sense of smell. These guards play on that idea.

Peter's Trial Before the High Priest's Maid (14:66-72)

14:66 one of the maids... The lack of power of Peter's judge, the maid, contrasts with that of Jesus' judge, the high priest. **14:68 he went out...** Peter looks to save his life instead of lose it (8:35). **and the rooster crowed.** This phrase follows "gateway" in many early manuscripts, but is not in most modern translations. It is the first of the two crowings that Jesus prophesied (14:30). **14:70 Galilean.** It seems to be understood that Peter is given away by his Galilean accent (Matthew 26:73). His accusers see Jesus' ministry as a Galilean affair. **14:71 invoke a curse...** Peter disassociates himself from Jesus as much as he can. **14:72 the cock crowed...** Peter realizes that Jesus' prophecy is fulfilled (14:30).

Unit XI

The Revelation of the Son of God

Introduction to Mark 15:1-39

As St. Polycarp entered the stadium, a voice from heaven said, "Be strong, Polycarp, and act manfully."

When he came before the Roman governor he was asked if he was the Bishop Polycarp. He admitted that he was, so the governor ordered him, "Swear by the spirit of Caesar; repent and say, 'Away with the atheists!'"

(Christians were called atheists because they did not accept the gods of the Roman Empire. Polycarp was told to swear that the emperor was a god. The Romans, on the other hand, were the true atheists as they did not accept the true God.)

Polycarp looked at the stadium, crowded with foolish pagans, and with a wave of his hand shouted, "Away with the atheists."

Angered, the governor became more insistent, "Swear the oath and I will let you go! Curse the Christ!"

Polycarp shot back, "For eighty-six years I have been his servant. He has never done me wrong. Why should I blaspheme my King, who saved me?"

Thoughtlessly the governor kept pressing, saying, "Swear by the spirit of Caesar!"

He answered, "You arrogantly suppose that I will swear by the spirit of Caesar. And you act like you are ignorant of who I am. Listen, I am a Christian. If you want to learn the truth of Christ, set a day for it and give me a hearing."

The governor didn't give him a hearing. Instead he had him burned at the stake before the angry stadium crowd. The year was 155 A.D. (For a fuller account read the second century document "The Martyrdom of Polycarp.")

St. Polycarp had an undying loyalty to Jesus. But his body suffered death for loyalty to Jesus. Jesus died for him, and Polycarp joined his death to Christ's.

In this section, we read of the death of Jesus. Know that millions of Christians have been killed for having borne the name of Christ. Know that many millions more have endured great sufferings because of their faithfulness to Jesus. All of them have drawn the strength to undergo such things from what you are about to read.

INDIVIDUAL STUDY
Read Mark 15:1-39 and then answer the following questions.

1. What is the main accusation leveled against Jesus?

2. Why does Pilate "wonder" at Jesus?

3. What does Pilate suspect of the chief priests?

4. Does Pilate consider Jesus to be innocent or guilty?

5. Whom does the crowd desire to be released?

6. What does the crowd lead Pilate to do?

7. What do the soldiers do to "honor" Jesus as King?

8. Who helps Jesus carry his cross?

9. Where is Jesus crucified?

10. What happens to Jesus' clothes?

11. What do the people who are near the cross tell Jesus to do?

12. Under what charge is Jesus crucified, and what title do the chief priests and scribes give him?

13. What happens at the sixth hour?

14. What happens when Jesus dies?

SHOP TALK:
Discuss these questions in your Bible study group.

GATHERING THE WOOD
(5 to 10 minutes)

- Begin with a prayer.

- Describe someone (perhaps a person in your family) who made sacrifices out of love for you.

BUILDING ON THE FOUNDATION (40 to 45 minutes)

Reread each passage before discussing it.

Jesus' Trial Before Pilate (15:1-5)
Pilate wonders at Jesus because he offers no defense for himself while the chief priests level many accusations against him. He realizes that Jesus is innocent and the accusing priests are the ones who are truly guilty. Which is better: to accuse others or to accuse yourself? Which is better: to excuse others or to excuse yourself?

The Crowd Rejects Jesus (15:6-15)
Pilate releases a guilty man to win popularity. He condemns an innocent man because of the crowd's thirst for blood. Why is popularity so attractive? How might people who follow fads and seek popularity end up crucifying Christ today?

The Crucifixion (15:16-32)
The soldiers and others mock and torture Jesus, but they unwittingly reveal the truth about him: Jesus really is the King of the Jews. What do you imagine went through the minds of those who mocked him?

The Death of Jesus (15:33-39)
Right up to his death, Jesus is abandoned and mocked without mercy. He bears it all with the greatest of dignity. In the end, one man stands converted by Jesus' death. This man is not a righteous man. In fact, he just took part in the greatest sin of all: the killing of God. Yet Jesus suffers and dies for this very man. What do you think of when you recall that Jesus died for love of you? What do you think of when you recall that it was because of your sins that he went to the cross?

APPLYING THE FINISH
(10 minutes)

It is good for the soul to reflect on the suffering and death of our Lord. Consider what Jesus did for love of you. What things can you do to express your love of Jesus?

During the closing prayer, thank Jesus for taking up his cross.

Alternative closing prayer: Pray the Chaplet of Divine Mercy or the Sorrowful Mysteries of the Rosary.

Explanations

Jesus' Trial Before Pilate (15:1-5)

15:1 held a consultation. This seems to be a meeting after the one in 14:53-65. **Pilate.** Pilate is the Rome-appointed governor of Palestine. He ruled from about 26 to 35 A.D. The Romans reserved to themselves the legal power to carry out a death sentence; therefore, the Jews turn him over to Pilate to be killed (10:33). **15:2 King of the Jews?** The chief priests bring this charge against Jesus to set him up as a political threat to Roman authority. **You have said so.** This strange response is an acceptance of the charge that Jesus is the Christ, the King, but it is also a rejection of the political threat charge. **15:3 many things.** Seeing that the main accusation does not convince Pilate, the priests heap many false accusations upon Jesus. **15:5 Pilate wondered.** Earlier, Jesus' words amazed people (1:27; 2:12; 10:24, 32; 12:17); now his silence does.

The Crowd Rejects Jesus (15:6-15)

15:6 feast. Passover time (14:12). **15:7 Barabbas.** A murderer in a revolt, Barabbas is a political hero to many Jews. "Barabbas" means "son of the father" (10:46; 14:36). Thus, he is a false messiah who comes "in Jesus' name" (13:6), but Jesus is the true Son of the Father (1:1). **15:9-10 Do you want...** Pilate wants to release Jesus, but he also wants the crowd to ask for him so as to embarrass the chief priests. **15:14 Crucify him.** The fickle crowd (10:48-49) switches from praises of Jesus (11:9-10) to calls for his death. **15:15 wishing to satisfy...** This is Pilate's only reason for going along with the crucifixion. **having scourged Jesus.** This scourging involves whips with several cords. Some cords have weights on the ends, while others have sharp pieces of glass and metal attached.

The Crucifixion (15:16-32)

15:17 purple cloak. Purple is the color of royalty. They mock Jesus' kingship. **15:19 with a reed.** The reed represents a king's scepter. **15:20 put his own...** This is for convenience until they gamble for his clothes (15:24). **15:21 Simon of Cyrene.** Since Jesus is apparently unable to physically carry his cross the whole way, the soldiers randomly select this man to carry it. His Jewish name and his Gentile town of origin reflect how Jews and Gentiles conspire to kill Jesus. **Alexander and Rufus.** With their father's name, these names are Jewish, Greek, and Latin, signifying that Jesus' crucifixion is for the whole world. Alexander and Rufus were probably known to Mark's original audience in Rome (Romans 16:13). **15:22 Golgotha...** One tradition states that this is Adam's burial spot and the skull is Adam's skull. The crucifixion is the reversal of Adam's sin (Genesis 3:1-19; Romans 5:12-21). **15:23 wine mingled with...** This is a bitter-tasting anesthetic. Jesus does not drink it (14:25). **15:24 his garments.** Jesus' clothes often showed his power and glory (5:27-31; 6:56; 9:3). Now they show his humility and suffering under evil. **casting lots.** This fulfills Psalm 22:18. **15:25 third hour.** About 9:00 a.m. **15:26 King of the Jews.** This is the charge under which he is condemned, despite Pilate's knowledge of his innocence (15:14). **15:27 two robbers...** They receive the positions of being at Jesus' right and left (10:40). **15:28 And the scripture was fulfilled which says, "He was reckoned with the transgressors."** This verse does not appear in some ancient manuscripts and so is left out of most modern translations. It quotes Isaiah 53:12, showing Jesus' identification with sin in his crucifixion. **15:29 wagging their heads.** This gesture expresses hatred (2 Kings 19:21). **Aha!** This also expresses hatred (Psalm 35:21). **destroy the temple...** They recall the accusation made against Jesus at the trial (14:58), and unwittingly point to his resurrection by the reference to rebuilding the Temple in three days. **15:30 save yourself...** See the note on 15:32. **15:31 He saved others.** They admit Jesus' power, but they still mock him. **15:32 Christ, the King of Israel.** The chief priests use these titles in a mocking way, but the words are true. "King of Israel" is a more traditional title for the Christ than "King of the Jews" (Zephaniah 3:15). **come down now**... They wrongly think that coming down would prove him to be the Christ. Staying on the cross will. **Those who were**... Jesus is mocked and abandoned by everyone around him. The sins of all are poured on to Jesus.

The Death of Jesus (15:33-39)

15:33 sixth hour. About noon. **darkness.** Light, representing the created universe, (Genesis 1:3) abandons Jesus on the cross. **ninth hour.** About 3:00 p.m. **15:34 Eloi, Eloi**... Jesus experiences abandonment even by his Father. Sin makes him completely alone. Jesus' words are the first line of Psalm 22. Quoting a Psalm's first line recalls the entire Psalm, which, in this case, is the prayer of the righteous sufferer, and it ends with words of trust and hope in God. **15:35 calling Elijah.** They misinterpret "Eloi" as the word for "Elijah." They assume Jesus calls for Elijah to come reveal the Christ (9:11-13; Malachi 4:5). **15:36 vinegar.** The vinegar would hasten death by asphyxiation (Psalm 69:21). **Wait, let us**... The vinegar is pulled away to give Elijah time to come before Jesus' death. The grammar suggests that the man who gets the vinegar says, "Wait...", but it is more reasonable to conclude that bystanders (15:35) speak the words (Matthew 27:48-49). **15:37 loud cry.** Demons cried out when Jesus cast them out (1:26; 9:26). By this cry Jesus exorcises the sins of the whole world. **breathed his last.** At his baptism, the Spirit (Breath) of God descended upon him (1:10). Now his life-breath goes forth from him. **15:38 curtain of the temple**... The temple curtain surrounds the central sanctuary that only the high priest can enter, and that only once a year, in a prayer of atonement for the people's sins (Leviticus 16:1-34). The curtain's tearing from top to bottom points to a divine cause. This ends the legitimacy of the Temple liturgy as Jesus fulfills the whole purpose of that liturgy (see the note on 14:63). Atonement from Jesus, the true high priest, is now available always. Furthermore, this recalls the rending of the heavens at Jesus' baptism (1:10). **15:39 centurion.** In Mark's Gospel, a Gentile is the first human to confess Jesus' divinity. **facing him.** The centurion stands opposite Jesus, in a position to properly judge him (12:41; 13:3). **this man was the Son of God.** He recognizes Jesus to be both human (man) and divine (Son of God). The full truth of Jesus (1:1) is revealed by the cross.

Unit XII

From the Dead

Introduction to Mark 15:40 - 16:20

When Jesus appeared to Saint Francis the second time, Francis was praying in a little church that was in shambles after years of neglect. After the Lord appeared to him the first time, Francis left a life of parties and the pursuit of worldly glory. In that first appearance, the Lord promised a mission to Francis. Francis eagerly wanted to know what that mission would be. In this rundown little church, the Lord gave him that mission. He said, "Francis, rebuild my church."

Francis took Jesus at his word. He began to rebuild the little church. Francis had taken on a life of extreme poverty, forsaking all material possessions in order to maximize his freedom in loving God and others. Because of that, he had to beg for bricks and supplies to rebuild the little church where Jesus had appeared to him.

Inspired by his example, many young men who had partied with Francis joined him in poverty and obedience to Christ. Together they worked to rebuild the little church.

They succeeded in rebuilding that church – but the Lord's words had a double meaning.

Francis and his companions traveled to Rome to get permission from the Pope to start a new religious order. At first, they were greeted with suspicion as many extremists wanted the Pope's blessing, and Francis' poorly dressed band looked extreme. So the Pope turned them away.

That night, the Pope had a dream. He saw the Church in the midst of an earthquake. The Church fell apart as it shook. Then a man stood up, stretched out his hands, and brought stability. The Pope recognized the man who saved the Church: Francis of Assisi.

The next day the Holy Father had Francis brought back, and he gave Francis' group approval to be a religious order. The Franciscans were born.

Immediately, the Franciscans set out to preach the Gospel to people who had forgotten it and to people who had never heard it. Men joined their ranks in great numbers. Many more responded in repentance and belief. Within a century they had revitalized the Church.

The mission Jesus gives the Apostles at the end of this Gospel still exists. Jesus sent them out to bring the Gospel to the whole world. The Church exists to continue that mission. Saint Francis stepped up when corruption, immorality, and indifference were rocking the Church. His love of God, his love of neighbor, and his willingness to be holy no matter what the cost have brought untold good to millions.

By Baptism and Confirmation, each one of us is commissioned to join that mission. When we encounter corruption, immorality, and indifference, we must respond with purity, integrity, and devoted obedience to the Lord God and the Church he founded.

INDIVIDUAL STUDY

Read Mark 15:40-16:20 and then answer the following questions.

1. Who are the women who witness Jesus' death?

2. What does Joseph of Arimathea do for Jesus?

3. Why does Pilate hesitate to grant Joseph's request?

4. Who are the women who witness Jesus' burial?

5. Who are the women who go to anoint Jesus?

6. When do the women go to the tomb?

7. What is the women's concern as they approach the tomb?

8. What do the women encounter when they enter the tomb?

9. How do the women react to the young man in white?

10. How do the disciples first hear of the resurrection?

11. What is the first thing Jesus does when he comes to the disciples?

12. When the disciples go out to preach, how does Jesus want the people to respond?

13. What does Jesus do after commissioning the Eleven?

14. What do the Eleven do after being commissioned by Jesus?

Shop Talk:

Discuss these questions in your Bible study group.

Gathering the Wood

(5 to 10 minutes)

• Begin with a prayer.

• Describe your experience when you were given a job, task, or responsibility that you thought was too much for you.

Building on the Foundation (40 to 45 minutes)

Reread each passage before discussing it.

The Burial of Jesus (15:40-47)

It took courage for Joseph of Arimathea to ask for Jesus' body. Showing sympathy for a condemned man could lead to one's own execution. How can a person give honor to Jesus at work, school, or at home?

The Empty Tomb (16:1-8)

The women courageously go to honor Jesus by anointing him, but they meet with the unexpected. An angel instructs them to tell the disciples and Peter about Jesus' resurrection. This new mission is a greater honor than anointing his body, but fear prevents them from carrying it out. It can be a fearful thing to give honor to Jesus publicly. What might a modern Christian fear when he gives honor to Jesus?

The Messengers to the Eleven (16:9-13)

Jesus sends three people to the disciples to tell them about his resurrection. The disciples believe none of them. What do you think of the fact that, when Jesus sends people on a mission, he does not guarantee that the mission will be successful? What good can come out of an "unsuccessful" mission?

The Commissioning of the Eleven (16:14-20)

After leading the disciples to repent of their sins and doubts, Jesus gives these eleven men the task of bringing the Gospel to all of creation. They are successful: they do preach everywhere, and Jesus does work signs to confirm their ministry. The mission of the apostles continues as new generations arise. What role do you want in this mission? What role is Jesus calling you to take in this mission? What will be a sign to you that God is working through you?

Applying the Finish

(10 minutes)

Telling others what the Gospel can do for them begins with seeing what the Gospel has done and is doing in you. What benefits have you received from this tour of the Gospel of Jesus Christ according to Saint Mark? What do you know about Jesus now that you want others to know?

During the closing prayer, thank Jesus for working in your life, and pray for one other person.

Alternative closing prayer: pray the Glorious Mysteries of the Rosary.

Explanations

The Burial of Jesus (15:40-47)

15:40 women looking on... The women's position is close enough to make them witnesses of Jesus' death, but far enough to prevent them from being a comfort to Jesus. **15:41 ministered to him.** Like Simon's mother-in-law ministered to him (1:31), many women assisted Jesus and the apostles in their needs. **15:42 evening had come...** The sabbath begins at sunset. The day of Preparation is the day before the sabbath. When "evening had come" must refer to the late afternoon, after 3:00 p.m., but before sunset. **15:43 Arimathea.** Arimathea was formerly called Ramathaim-zophim (1 Samuel 1:1). Samuel, whom God chose to anoint the King of Israel (1 Samuel 10:1; 16:12-13), came from there. Joseph comes now to anoint the new King of Israel. **respected member...** Joseph could not prevent Jesus' condemnation at the council's proceedings (14:64; 15:1), but he now stands up in faith and courage to minister to Jesus. **15:44 Pilate wondered.** Often men hung on the cross for days before dying. The torture which Jesus endured prior to the crucifixion hastened his death. **15:46 linen shroud.** See the note on 14:52. **15:47 Mary Magdalene...** Two women who witnessed his death witness his burial. Their certainty of Jesus' death makes their testimony to the resurrection more credible.

The Empty Tomb (16:1-8)

16:1 sabbath was past. Now they can anoint Jesus' body (part of the burial customs), as the sabbath duty to rest has passed. **16:2 first day...** Sunday. This foreshadows the shift of the Lord's Day from the sabbath to Sunday, as it is the first day of the new creation (Genesis 1) and the day of the resurrection. **sun had risen.** This hints that the "Son" has risen. Throughout Christian history, the rising of the sun has been looked upon as a symbol of Christ's resurrection. **16:3 Who will roll...** The disciples are too afraid to go to the tomb to help. **16:5 young man...** The young man is not identified. Their amazement and his white robe indicate his heavenly origin (9:3). See the note on 14:52. **16:6 He has risen.** The young man (angel) gives testimony to Jesus' resurrection since none of the disciples were faithful enough to witness the actual event (see the notes on 5:37, 40). **16:7 disciples and Peter.** This message to the disciples shows Jesus' desire to forgive them. Peter's sin and restoration is highlighted as he is singled out. **Galilee.** This return to Galilee invites the reader to review Jesus' ministry in the light of the cross and resurrection. **you will see him.** The proof of the resurrection would have come to the disciples in Galilee, but their disobedience will bring the proof to them earlier (16:14). **16:8 they went out...** Fear prevents the women from fulfilling the angel's command.

The Messengers to the Eleven (16:9-13)

16:9-20 Now... 16:9-20 is missing in some manuscripts. It has long been suspected that these verses were not written by Mark. The Church, however, has always considered them to be authentic. **Mary Magdalene...** Jesus goes first to this "least one" (9:35-37), who had been saved from seven demons, and gives her a mission of evangelization (like the one in 5:19-20). **16:11 when they heard...** They have ears to hear, but do not hear (4:9, 23). **16:12 in another form.** Jesus' resurrected body is a transfigured one (9:2-3) that can appear in different forms and manners.

The Commissioning of the Eleven (16:14-20)

16:14 eleven. They are called the "eleven" instead of the "twelve" (3:14; 6:7) because Judas Iscariot is no longer with them. upbraided them... When Jesus came, he preached repentance and belief in the kingdom of God (1:15). Jesus' preaching after the resurrection is the same as before: he calls for the disciples to repent and believe. 16:15 Go into all... Having called them to repentance and faith, Jesus commissions them to carry out his ministry to the whole of creation (13:10). He wants every place to be filled with the kingdom of God; he wants every person to hear and accept the Gospel. 16:16 He who believes... This mirrors Jesus' call to belief and repentance (1:15). Baptism is the Sacrament of belief and repentance. Jesus requires it for salvation. he who does not... Baptism is not repeated here because it's understood. The people who do not believe are not going to repent and receive baptism. 16:17 these signs... The miraculous signs are God's testimony to the truth of the Gospel and to his love for his disciples. 16:18 drink any deadly thing. This is the only one of these signs that does not appear in any New Testament account of the apostles' ministry. 16:19 Lord Jesus. "Lord" means God (12:38-40). sat down... To sit at the right hand of God is to share God's authority. Jesus is his "right hand man." 16:20 they went forth... They obey Jesus and preach everywhere (13:10; 16:15). Amen. This final word means "It is true," and certifies Mark's intention to pass on what is true and worthy of faith.

Appendix 1:
Introduction to the Bible

Imagine you were given up for adoption at birth and grew up never knowing your father. One day you answer the door and find a man standing before you. He states his name and reveals that he is your father.

At that point you have to decide what you'll do. You can believe him at his word. You can invite the man in and question him. Or you can slam the door in his face. You can react with hope, curiosity, or even anger. But you cannot ignore him and say that you really don't care.

Apathy is impossible here. Why? Because inside each of us is the desire to know the ones who created us. It doesn't matter if you entertain that desire by inviting the man in or if you deny it by slamming the door in his face. Either way, you show the desire's existence. Hope and curiosity show that desire. Anger shows the frustration of that desire. We all want to know the ones who made us.

Please pardon this limping analogy, but something similar happens with divine revelation. Through revelation God has walked into human history and announced that he is God, Creator, and Father.

Now you must decide how you'll respond. You can believe him at his word. You can investigate the claims to see if they are true. Or you can reject him and his claims. But you cannot truthfully say that you don't care, because inside you is a desire to know the God who created you.

Those who say they simply don't care about God often use apathy to mask their fear. What might they be afraid of? The relationship. All significant relationships are life-changing. Becoming a husband, a mother, or a best friend all affects life's daily routines.

Having a relationship with God changes life even more. A relationship with God involves a person's entire being. People often act apatheticly towards God because they fear how God will change their lives.

To gain your trust, the father at the door must have strong credentials. The earthly father may have a birth certificate, knowledge that only he could have, or a strong resemblance to you.

But what about the Heavenly Father? What kind of credentials must he have? Like the earthly father, God wants to reveal who he is and the relationship he desires to have with us. God's credentials will show us who he is and how to have this relationship. His credentials are his words and deeds. The Bible presents God's credentials to us.

If we are to believe God, his words will have to strike us as true. His plans for us will have to fulfill our deepest needs. His deeds will have to show that he has the power to make his hopes for us a reality. He will have to prove that he can do what only a God can do. He will have to perform miracles, miracles that show who he is and his power to save us.

Studying the Bible is a marvelous adventure because it's an examination of God's credentials. Of course, coming to faith in God involves more than studying the Bible, but such study is one of the best ways to come to know God on a personal level.

Now we know what the purpose of the Bible is, but what's inside the Bible? We call the Bible a book but really it is more like a library, since there are actually 73 books in the Bible.

The Bible has two major parts. The first part is the Old Testament, which includes 46 books. These books teach us about what God did from the creation of the world up to the time just before the arrival of Jesus Christ. (Jeremiah 31:31-32)

During the time of the Old Testament, God made many covenants with the people of Israel. These covenants made the Israelites God's chosen people. The word "covenant" is often translated as "testament," so we have come to refer to the covenants prior to Jesus as being the "Old Testament." (More accurately the covenant referred to by "Old Testament" is the covenant God made with Moses. The other Old Testament covenants are generally viewed in relation to the Mosaic covenant.) The Old Testament is "Old" because God gave us a new covenant, a new testament, through Jesus Christ.

The New Testament, the second part of the Bible, is a collection of 27 books that give us the life and teachings of Jesus Christ. Jesus commissioned twelve men to tell everyone about the covenant God offers them through Jesus Christ. These twelve men are called apostles ("apostle" means "one who is sent"). Through their preaching and their writings they transmitted the Gospel – the good news of the new covenant – to a great many people. The apostles' writings, and the writings that received their approval, were gathered into the New Testament.

Who wrote the Bible, God or men? We understand the authorship of the 73 books of the Bible in two ways. In one way, we recognize these books as the work of various men writing over a span of about 1300 years. In the other way – and this is the more important one – we recognize them as being authored by God.

God inspired the various writings to be written. This is more than the beauty of a woman inspiring a man to compose a love poem. The words the Bible uses to describe it is that God breathed the words of Scripture (2 Timothy 3:16). That's what "inspired by God" literally means. But at the same time the human writers weren't just secretaries writing whatever they heard God say. Instead, they fully applied their minds to the work of writing so that the books were truly their work as well.

Still, one may ask how both God and men can be the authors of the Bible. The key to resolving this seeming difficulty is the ancient teaching that God's grace perfects nature rather than destroys it. That means that when God sent his Spirit to the human authors, he truly empowered those men to make full use of their minds to write. And by the power of grace, he elevated their minds, without coercion, to desire to write what God desired to have written.

The main point is that, even though the Bible has many human authors, God unifies it by authoring all its books through the mystery of inspiration.

Why is the Bible sometimes called Scripture? The Bible is called "Scripture" (which means "writing") because it is the Writing of God. Scripture is called the "Bible" (which means "book") because it is the Book of God.

Where can I learn more? For more about the Bible and divine revelation read the *Catechism of the Catholic Church* (CCC) 50-141, and the Vatican II document *Dogmatic Constitution on Divine Revelation*.

Appendix 2:
Quick and Easy Guide to
Bible and Catechism References

Bible References

Bible references make it easy to find things in the Bible quickly. They tell us which book, chapter, and verse to look for. (The Bible actually contains 73 books, so it's important to identify the book.) Most biblical books are divided into chapters. Chapters are divided into verses. Verses are not the same thing as sentences, but they're close.

Example: Mark 10:45

"Mark" is the biblical book. "10" is the chapter. "45" directs us to the verse. The number before the colon (:) is the chapter reference. The number after the colon tells us the verse.

Below are examples of references. Go ahead and find them in your Bible.

Ephesians 5:21-32

This reference includes all verses from 21 through 32.

Isaiah 52:13-53:12

This reference covers verses from more than one chapter, specifically all verses from 52:13 to 53:12.

Mark 4:9, 23

A comma is used when referring to two or more verses from the same chapter.

John 3:16; 1 John 5:3

A semi-colon is used when the references do not come from the same chapter or from the same book. This example includes verses from two different books (John and 1 John).

Mark 15:39b

The letter indicates that only part of the verse is being referenced. The letter "a" refers to the first part of the verse, letter "b" to the second, etc.

Catechism References

References to the *Catechism of the Catholic Church* are a little different. Example: *CCC* 1644-1651. "*CCC*" stands for the *Catechism of the Catholic Church*. In modern Church documents, such as the Catechism, the paragraphs are numbered. 1644-1651 refers to the paragraphs with those numbers.

Quotes and More

Mostly, people use references when they quote the Bible or the Catechism. Sometimes people use them to back up a statement. Look up these two examples of other times.

Jesus predicts his death and his rising three times (Mark 8:31; 9:31; 10:33).

The phrase "Most High God" is often used by Gentiles in the Bible to reverently speak of God (Genesis 14:19; Daniel 3:26).

Appendix 3:
The Controversy About Mark

Before the Controversy

Until the late 18th century, Mark received considerably less attention than any of the three other Gospels. Scholars studied Matthew more than Mark because it was longer, made more theological points, and was written by an eyewitness. And since nearly all the passages in Mark are also in Matthew and Luke, there was little reason to write a commentary on Mark.

In the past two centuries Mark has received a great deal more attention. Why the change? The reason stems from a modern theory of the origin of the Synoptics.

The vast similarities between Matthew, Mark, and Luke has led them to be called the Synoptic Gospels or the Synoptics. ("Synoptic" means "seeing together.") John's Gospel is not one of the Synoptics because it takes a very different approach to presenting the ministry of Christ and relates only a few of the same events as the others.

Since the Synoptics share so much of the same material, churchmen have long tried to determine how Matthew, Mark, and Luke influenced each other's writing. The early Church Fathers taught how each of the Gospels came from the Apostles: Matthew and John were both Apostles and wrote about what they had seen; Mark drew on the Apostle Peter; Luke drew on the Apostle Paul among other sources. In the fifth century, St. Augustine used this tradition and a laborious examination of the Synoptics to conclude that Matthew indeed wrote first; that Mark took Matthew and abbreviated his work; and that Luke drew upon Mark, Matthew, and other sources.

It is uncertain how Mark used both Matthew's Gospel and Peter's preaching in forming his Gospel. It may have been that Peter had a copy of Matthew and used it to help organize his preaching. In this way Mark's writing could have been heavily influenced by Matthew, while remaining essentially the written form of Peter's preaching about Jesus' words and deeds.

The Controversy Begins

This traditional understanding was universally held until the 18th century. Late in the 18th century, some Protestant critics in Germany began to reject the testimony of the Church Fathers concerning the origins of the Gospels. Instead, they decided to look solely at the texts themselves to determine when and how they were written. Using this approach they decided that Mark wrote the first Gospel (the Marcan priority theory). They thought the differences between the Synoptics were best explained by thinking Matthew and Luke edited and expanded upon Mark. This declaration that Mark was the first Gospel led to a new emphasis on Mark. Currently the majority of scholars consider Mark to be the first Gospel written.

Two Arguments in Favor of Marcan Priority

There are two very important arguments in favor of Marcan priority. They are the Argument from Expansion and the Argument from Internal Order.

The Argument from Expansion comes from the idea that people like to add details and other information to stories and documents as they are passed from one person to the next. For example, a mother may write a Christmas newsletter about her family and then pass it on to her husband to see if he had any comments on it. He might tell her he'd like more said about Timmy's first basketball season, his own recent promotion, and his wife's first trip in a hot air balloon. The idea here is that a second contributor is more likely to expand the writing than to reduce it. Since Matthew and Luke cover most of what Mark wrote and add a lot more, then it's reasonable to suspect that Mark may have been the first written, and the others simply expanded upon his work.

This argument is never offered as definite proof that Mark wrote first, but scholars see it as making Marcan priority more probable than the traditional explanation. The reason it's not seen as a proof is because exceptions to this pattern are common, and it's easy to see how Mark may

have simply decided to abbreviate the lengthy Matthew.

The Argument from Internal Order is generally seen as the most powerful argument in favor of Marcan priority. This argument is very complex, and too lengthy to be described in detail here. For those who are interested, the *New Jerome Biblical Commentary* has a relatively brief description of the argument in the article entitled "Synoptic Problem" (there the argument is called the "argument from order").

The basic idea of this argument is that, when one looks at the order of passages in Matthew, Mark, and Luke and how their order differs from one another, the best way to explain their similarities and differences is by positing that Mark wrote first and that Matthew and Luke both independently revised and expanded upon Mark. This argument, although complex, is quite strong. Traditional replies to this argument – necessarily getting complex themselves – follow on the basic idea that Mark abbreviated and reordered the passages in Matthew, and that Luke, who may very well have had access to both Matthew and Mark, followed Matthew's order when he thought it best to do so, Mark's order when he thought it best to do so, and his other sources when he thought it best to do so.

An Underlying Motive

There are many reasons why scholars and teachers have accepted the Marcan priority theory. Undoubtedly, most sincerely believe that it is the most reasonable explanation of the origins of the Gospels. I have no doubt that what I'm about to say does not reflect how a great many people came to accept the Marcan priority theory. At the same time, I think it's valuable to be aware of a powerful motive for accepting the Marcan priority theory: the consequences of Marcan priority tend to weaken support for the Pope's authority.

Probably the most important Scripture passage regarding the Pope's authority is Matthew 16:13-20, where Jesus gives St. Peter the keys to the kingdom of heaven. Since the Popes are the successors of St. Peter, wielding his authority, and since Protestants reject the authority of the Pope, the interpretation of this passage has been the subject of much controversy. In Mark's version of this event (Mark 8:27-30) there is no reference to Jesus bestowing authority on Peter.

Under the theory of Marcan priority, Matthew took Mark's account of this event and added the bestowal of authority upon Peter. This led many scholars to doubt that Jesus ever said these words to Peter. They think that Matthew made them up in order to emphasize the Church's importance. If this is true, then the Pope's authority is not based on an actual historical event, but on the imaginative theology of an anonymous Christian late in the first century. Therefore, this theory holds an attraction for those who would undermine the Pope's authority.

It must be noted that not all who hold Marcan priority consider themselves to be opponents of the papacy. Assuming that they are can lead to more misunderstandings and harm efforts to unify the Church. But it is still helpful to understand that some of Marcan priority's popularity stems from anti-papal feelings.

Problems with the New Thinking

Although there are many strong arguments in favor of Marcan priority, there are many serious difficulties that accompany it. Five such difficulties are listed below.

One, the Marcan priority theory ignores the historical evidence regarding the origins of the Gospel. Every early Church Father who said anything about the authorship of or the order of the Synoptics, says that Matthew wrote first, not Mark. This is either true or false. If true, then the theory of Marcan priority is false. If Marcan priority is false, then we must ask why the Church Fathers said what they did with such frequency, and without anybody opposing them. There were many disputed issues in the early Church, but this was not one of them. I have not found a convincing explanation for how the Fathers could have gotten it so wrong, if indeed Marcan priority is true.

Two, the theory calls into question the authenticity of the Gospel of Matthew. The Church admitted the Gospels into the New Testament in large part because they came from the Apostles, or from men approved by the Apostles. This theory maintains that the author of Matthew was not one of the Apostles, as Tradition teaches. The reasoning often given is that there would be no need for an Apostle, who had been an eyewitness to Jesus' ministry, to more or less copy Mark and another document, while only adding a few other passages. Therefore, it seems unlikely to them that Matthew was written by the Apostle Matthew. If Matthew wasn't the author, then one of the biggest reasons the Church included the Gospel of Matthew in the New Testament is gone.

Three, the Marcan priority theory teaches that the non-Marcan material that Matthew and Luke share comes from a document called "Q" ("Q" stands for "Quelle," a German word meaning "source") – but there is no historical evidence that this document ever existed. No scraps of Q have ever been found and no early Church Father ever makes reference to the kind of document scholars say Q was.

Four, many scholars who have extensively studied the relationships of the Synoptics have determined that the traditional understanding, that Matthew wrote first, does a far better job of explaining the relationships of the Synoptics than the Marcan priority theory does.

Five, the Pontifical Biblical Commission, on June 26, 1912, stated that without any historical evidence to support it, Catholics cannot hold the Marcan priority theory.

Since the Pontifical Biblical Commission issued its statements early in the 20th century, the Church has issued many teachings regarding biblical studies. None of these teachings explicitly reversed or rescinded the Commission's statements. However, by using ambiguous language at certain times, the Magisterium (the Church's official teaching office) gave tacit permission to Catholic scholars to not be strictly bound by the Commission's statement. Consequently, even though the Commission's statement is still "on the books," many biblical scholars largely ignore it. Presumably in order to encourage open dialogue, the Magisterium is not expected to issue any statements on this matter in the foreseeable future.

If you intend to study or debate this subject further, please be respectful of others' arguments and perspectives. But do not allow your respect of others lead you to sacrifice your pursuit of the truth. And always be prepared to accept the Magisterium's definitive judgment on the matter. Remember the words from the "Prayer of St. Francis" – "It is better to understand than to be understood."

Map of Israel in Jesus' Day

(All Scripture references are from Mark.)

Arimathea (15:43). Arimathea, formerly called Ramathaim-zophim, is 20 miles northwest of Jerusalem in Judea.

Bethsaida (6:45; 8:22). This town on the northeast shore of the Sea of Galilee has both Jewish and Gentile residents.

Bethphage and Bethany (11:1, 11, 12; 14:3). These two small towns are close to the east side of Jerusalem.

Beyond the Jordan (3:8; 10:1). The Trans-Jordan is Gentile territory to the east of the Jordan River. It once was territory held by the Israelites.

Caesarea Philippi (8:27) This mostly Gentile city is well north of the Sea of Galilee.

Capernaum (1:21; 2:1; 9:33). Capernaum is a very significant city lying on a major trade route on the north shore of the Sea of Galilee.

Cyrene (15:21). This is a large city in North Africa with a large Jewish population.

Dalmanutha (8:10). The exact location of this Jewish region is uncertain. It is probably on the southwestern side of the Sea of Galilee.

Decapolis (5:20; 7:31). The Decapolis is an association of ten Gentile cities mainly to the southeast of the Sea of Galilee. Parts of it are to the northeast of Galilee.

Galilee (1:9, 14, 28, 39; 3:7; 6:21; 9:30; 14:28, 70; 15:41; 16:7). Galilee is northern Israel and is populated mostly by Jews. Jesus focuses his early ministry here.

Gennesaret (6:53). This is a small region on the northwest side of the Sea of Galilee.

Gerasa (5:1, 14). This is Gentile territory to the southeast of the Sea of Galilee. Gerasa is an influential town 30 miles southeast of the Sea.

Gethsemane (14:32). This garden is on the Mount of Olives.

Golgotha (15:22). This hill is just outside Jerusalem's walls.

Idumea (3:8). This is Gentile territory south of Judea, once held by the Israelites.

Jericho (10:46). Jericho is a Jewish city in Judea northeast of Jerusalem.

Jerusalem (1:5; 3:8; 7:1; 10:32-33; 11:1, 11, 15, 27; 15:41). Jerusalem, the Holy City, is set on a mountain in Judea. King David made it the capital of Israel. David's son, King Solomon (1 Kings 6:1-37) built the Temple here. All the action from 11:1 on takes place in or near Jerusalem.

Jordan River (1:5, 9). This forms a natural eastern border to Israel. The people of Israel miraculously crossed this river to enter the Promised Land (Joshua 3:1-4:24).

Judea (1:5; 3:7; 10:1; 13:14). Judea is the southern region of Israel (the Holy Land) and has the highest concentration of Jews.

Mount of Olives (11:1; 13:3; 14:26). This mountain is east of the Jerusalem Temple.

Nazareth (1:9, 24; 6:1; 14:67; 16:6). Nazareth is an obscure town in Galilee west of the Sea of Galilee.

Samaria (not mentioned in Mark). This is the non-Jewish central region between Judea and Galilee.

Sea of Galilee (1:16; 2:13; 3:7; 4:1; 5:1, 13, 21; 6:47-49; 7:31). Much of the action in Mark takes place near or on this Sea. This Sea is really a large lake on the eastern side of Galilee. The Jordan River flows from it.

Syrophoenicia (7:26). Syria and Phoenicia are northern Gentile regions.

Tyre and Sidon (3:8; 7:24, 31). These are Gentile towns to the north of Israel on the Mediterranean coast. At one time Tyre was under Israelite control.

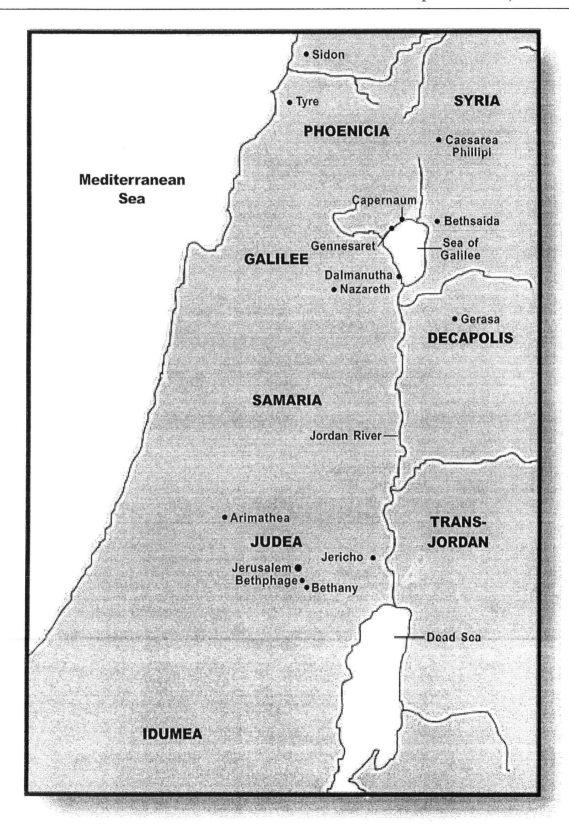

Sidon

Tyre

SYRIA

PHOENICIA

Caesarea
Phillipi

**Mediterranean
Sea**

Capernaum

Bethsaida

Gennesaret

Sea of
Galilee

GALILEE

Dalmanutha

Nazareth

Gerasa

DECAPOLIS

SAMARIA

Jordan River

Arimathea

**TRANS-
JORDAN**

JUDEA

Jericho

Jerusalem
Bethphage   Bethany

Dead Sea

IDUMEA

Recommended Resources

Extra Copies of The Lion's Roar
Additional copies are available via Amazon.com and Jimhornecker.wordpress.com

Audio Explanations and Commentary
This engaging 3-CD series with Steve Wood and James Hornecker covers the 12 units of *The Lion's Roar*, providing additional insights and rich commentary on St. Mark's Gospel as well as a stimulating discussion on key Marcan passages and the controversy about Mark. This set is a perfect accompaniment to the book. To purchase, contact the author via Jimhornecker.wordpress.com.

The Lion's Roar Leader's Guide On CD-ROM
This CD-ROM is designed for small group Bible study leaders, classroom teachers and homeschool teachers. It includes the answers to all the Individual Study questions, a multiple choice test, and test answers. To purchase, contact the author via Jimhornecker.wordpress.com.

Online
Check out the discussion about Gospel of Mark topics at Jimhornecker.wordpress.com.

Made in the USA
Middletown, DE
17 September 2015